JOHN

Personal Reflections Series

BETH MOORE

JOHN

90 DAYS WITH THE BELOVED DISCIPLE

B&H
PUBLISHING GROUP

NASHVILLE, TENNESSEE

JOHN

John: 90 Days with *The Beloved Disciple*

Copyright © 2008 by Beth Moore

All Rights Reserved

978-0-8054-4812-2

B&H Publishing Group

Nashville, Tennessee

BHPublishingGroup.com

Dewey Decimal Classification: 248.84

John, Apostle \ Spiritual Life

Printed in the USA

1 2 3 4 5 6 7 8 9   12 11 10 09 08

To my new son, Curt

If I could have looked the world over for a partner for my firstborn,
I would have chosen you. No need. God already had.

My dear Curt, as I wrote this book, I often thought about how very much
you favor the apostle John. You are a true man of vision, driven to the *Logos* by
godly affection. You are the essence of a deeply beloved disciple. I love you.

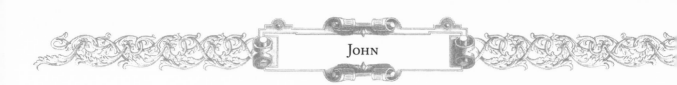

John

WHAT WAS FROM THE BEGINNING,
what we have heard, what we have seen with our eyes,
what we have observed, and have touched with our hands,
concerning the Word of life—that life was revealed,
and we have seen it and we testify and declare to you
the eternal life that was with the Father and was
revealed to us—what we have seen and heard
we also declare to you, so that you may have
fellowship along with us; and indeed
our fellowship is with the Father
and with His Son Jesus Christ.
We are writing these things
so that our joy may
be complete.

FIRST JOHN 1:1–4

INTRODUCTION

John, the youngest of Christ's apostles, would certainly qualify as one of the most fascinating characters in Scripture. He anonymously penned the Gospel that most people consider their favorite. He identified himself only as the "disciple whom Jesus loved." He took the other Gospel accounts of Jesus the Messiah and wrote as if to say, "You've heard what Jesus did, now let me show you who He really was." Thus John shows us the cosmic Christ who created the world, died to redeem it, and lives to reclaim it.

The apostle John's life includes unbelievable moments of courage and greatness. Of the twelve, only John stayed near for the crucifixion, and he became the recipient of the capstone of Scripture: the Revelation. He walked in the inner circle with Jesus to places like the Mount of Transfiguration and the resurrection chamber of Jairus' daughter (Luke 8:51), yet between those mountaintops John experienced many long years when others stood in the limelight. From this disciple we gain an intimate and personal perspective of both Jesus and of a beloved follower.

So come along with me for a wonderful journey with the apostle John. Together we'll scale the heights and plumb the depths. My prayer is that in the process we'll come to identify personally with this long-lived follower of Christ. In the end, I hope you'll make the discovery that he did so long ago—the discovery that affection counts for more than ambition. That loving and being loved by Jesus matters more than all that the world can obtain or contain.

John was free to love because he was so utterly convinced that he was loved himself. "We have come to know and to believe the love that God has for us. God is love, and the one who remains in love remains in God, and God remains in him" (1 John 4:16). Leave it to John to pen these words. How differently would each follower live if we characterized ourselves above all else as the beloved disciple of Jesus Christ? Our water would be turned to wine and our joy made complete. Oh, how we would long for the day when we see our Bridegroom face-to-face—the living, breathing Son of God!

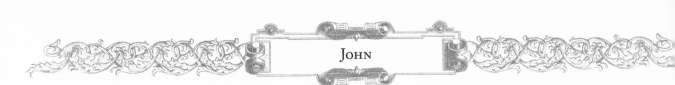

I can't wait to see why God has invited me along on this journey. I have no preconceived notions. No idea where this study is going. An unknown adventure lies ahead of me as surely as it does for you. I can't wait to see all the stops we'll make and all the keepsakes we'll pick up along the way. But when all is said and done, I have a feeling we will learn much about identity. Whose? Christ's and two of His very important disciples. One we'll meet in the pages of this book. The other you can meet in the nearest mirror.

I'm so glad you've joined me. Let's have a blast in the Word of God. I hope you love your journey, because I love you. And in whatever way Christ applies the truths of these pages to your precious life, let Him romance you along the way.

DAY 1

The Little Brother

Before You Begin

Read Matthew 4:18–22

Stop and Consider

Going on from there, He saw two other brothers, James the son of Zebedee, and his brother John. They were in a boat with Zebedee their father, mending their nets. (v. 21)

What were you doing when Jesus first came to you? What ordinary things occupied your time and attention? _____

_____

_____

_____

In what ways might your nature and background be similar to John's? Or in what ways could your two experiences not possibly be any more unlike? _____

_____

_____

_____

The people we will come to know together in this book were Jews at a time when Judaism had perhaps never been more Jewish. By this expression I mean that although they were under Roman rule, they enjoyed significant freedom to live out their culture. They were firmly established in their land and had their temple. Every sect of religious life was functioning at full throttle: the Pharisees, the Sadducees, and the teachers of the law, to name only a few.

Life in the Galilean villages of Capernaum and Bethsaida must have seemed light-years away from the hub of religious life and Herod's temple in Jerusalem, but one thing varied little from Hebrew to Hebrew: YHWH was life. Provider, Sustainer, Sovereign Creator of all things. (YHWH is the divine name of God, never pronounced by the Jews; in English it is often referred to as Yahweh or Jehovah.) To them, to have little thought of God was to have little thought at all.

Our John the apostle came from the rural land to the north. If the more sophisticated Jew in the Holy City thought the simple settlers on the Sea of Galilee envied him, he was sorely mistaken. Neither was without the inevitable troubles that make living part of life. Each had his preferences. Each had a point of view. One awakened to the brilliance of the sun dancing off the gleaming walls of the temple. The other saw the sun strolling on the surface of the lake. A fisherman would have been hard to convince that the glory of God dwelled more powerfully in a building made of stone than in a bright pink and purple sunset over the Sea of Galilee. I know this for a fact. I live with a fisherman.

Two pairs of sons grew up not far from each other on the northern tip of the Sea of Galilee. Four pairs of feet earned their calluses on the pebbles of a familiar shore. From the time their sons were knee-high to them, Zebedee and Jonah were responsible not only for making sure their rambunctious offspring didn't drown but also for harnessing their insatiable curiosity with their trades. The fathers were the walking day-care centers for their sons, and their sons' mothers would be expecting them home in one piece before dusk or after a long night of fishing.

Peter, Andrew, James, and John. They were trees planted by streams of water being raised to bring forth their own fruit in season (Ps. 1:3). If those fathers had only known what would become of their sons, I wonder if they would have raised them any differently.

Come to think of it, I doubt it. They were simple men with one simple goal: to teach their sons all they knew.

Our task is to piece together what our protagonist's life might have been like in childhood and youth before a Lamb came and turned it upside down. We first meet John on the pages of the New Testament in Matthew 4:21. There we read that the fishing boat contained "James the son of Zebedee, and his brother John." Scholars are almost unanimous in their assumption that John was the younger brother of James. In the earlier references, he is listed after his brother, James, which was often an indication of birth order in Scripture and other ancient Eastern literature.

> The firstborn was a leader in the family, commanding a certain amount of respect. John? He was just the little brother.

In their world, if any name existed more common than James (a hellenized form of *Iakob* or Jacob), it was John. Since the family used the Hebrew language, they actually called him Jehohanan. It may sound a little fancier, but the name was as common as could be. I don't get the feeling James and John were the kinds of boys about whom the neighbors mused, "I can't wait to see what they'll turn out to be. Mark my word. They'll be something special!" Those who watched them grow up assumed the sons of Zebedee would be fisherman. Just like their father.

If we're right and James was the older brother, he held the coveted position in the family birth order. Special rights and privileges belonged to him as well as a birthright that assured him a double portion of his father's estate. The firstborn was a leader in the family, commanding a certain amount of respect for a position he did nothing to earn. John? He was just the little brother.

Most of us have experienced the ambiguity of being known by little more than our relationship to someone else. I can remember feeling lost in a whole line of siblings growing up. I have fond memories of my mother calling me every name in our big family but mine. I often grinned while she scrambled for the right one and then, exasperated, finally would say, "If I'm looking at you, I'm talking to you!" I'd giggle, "Yes, ma'am!" and run off while she was still doing her best to remember what my name was.

Some things about parenting must be universal. Surely Zebedee looked straight at Jehohanan and accidentally called him Iakob at times. If so, would young John have been the type to let it go unnoticed, or might he have said, "Abba! I am Jehohanan!" These are thoughts I love to explore imaginatively when studying a character.

Either way John was no doubt accustomed to being Zebedee's other son and James's little brother. However common his name, the meaning was extraordinary: "God has been gracious."[1] Growing up on the shore of Jesus' favorite sea, John had no idea at this point just how gracious God had been. He would soon get a glimpse.

How have you been identified by your relationship with others? In what ways has this been a blessing in your life? In what ways, though, has it seemed limiting or restrictive, making you feel misunderstood, as though you can't be yourself? _____

_____

_____

_____

_____

PRAYING GOD'S WORD TODAY

Lord, I am awed by the many times in Scripture when the gospel writers, in crafting their divinely inspired narratives, wrote the words, "Jesus came . . ." To the home of a synagogue official whose daughter awaited healing (Matt. 9:23). To the town where Zacchaeus lived, awaiting a new heart (Luke 19:5). To disciples cowering behind closed doors following His death and resurrection, awaiting belief (John 20:19). I praise you today, Lord Jesus, for coming to us . . . for coming to me. _____

DAY 2

Amazing!

BEFORE YOU BEGIN

Read Luke 5:1–11

STOP AND CONSIDER

He fell at Jesus' knees and said, "Go away from me, because I'm a sinful man, Lord!"
For he and all those with him were amazed at the catch of fish they took. (vv. 8–9)

When was the last time Christ amazed you? How did it come about? What did it change about your or someone else's circumstances? _____

_____

_____

Our natural tendency is to lose our sense of wonder over time. But why? What causes the human heart and spirit to find God less awe-inspiring than He actually is? _____

_____

_____

_____

At the time when Andrew, Peter, James, and John were casting their nets into the Sea of Galilee, a vigorous fishing industry was booming all over the lake. Many villages populated the shores of this body of water. Not only was it the food basket of the region; the sight was breathtaking. It still is. The surrounding hills cup the lake like water in the palm of a large hand. I've seen with my own eyes how the early spring sunrise hangs lazily in the clinging winter mist. Since the first time I saw the Sea of Galilee, I understood why Christ seemed to favor the villages near its shore over the metropolis of Jerusalem.

Bethsaida lies at the northern tip where the Jordan River feeds the lake. The name Bethsaida means "house of fishing,"[2] and it lived up to its name. We know for a fact that Andrew and Peter were from Bethsaida, and we can safely assume Zebedee also raised his sons in the village, since they were all partners. As we will soon discover, at some point Andrew and Peter moved to nearby Capernaum where Peter lived with his wife and mother-in-law (Mark 1:21, 29). We don't know for certain which of the two villages housed James and John at this point in their lives, but we do know they all continued to work together.

Obviously Zebedee was the one who owned the fishing enterprise. We read in Mark 1:20 that James and John "left their father Zebedee in the boat with the hired men." While I don't want to intimate that Zebedee was wealthy (since few villagers were), we'd probably be mistaken to think him poor. The reference to the hired servants tells us that he owned his own business and was profitable enough to have servants in addition to two healthy and able sons. Both boats might easily have been in his ownership. Peter and Andrew could have fished from one (which was considered theirs in Luke 5:3) while a little farther away (Mark 1:19) James and John fished from another.

God wisely equipped us with four Gospels because we learn far more from hearing several accounts of anything especially noteworthy. The facts one writer included may not have been noted by another because each point of view was tinted by the individual's perspective and priorities. While writing *Jesus the One and Only*, I learned I could almost always expect Luke to be a little more specific than the other Gospel writers, which made perfect sense to me. He was a doctor, and a good doctor pays attention to details. You'll find this principle to hold true in the passage at hand.

Christ has a divinely uncanny ability to waltz right into a life and turn it upside down, inside out, and every which way but loose.

In his fifth chapter, Luke recorded the call of Peter, Andrew, James, and John. Simon Peter told Jesus that they had fished all night. Obviously our little band of fisherman worked the graveyard shift at times. I can only think of one thing worse than fishing in the cold. That would be not catching anything. It happens to the best of fisherman. When it happens to my husband, Keith, I always ask him the typical sanguine woman question: "But did you have fun with your friends anyway?" My personality is given to the philosophy that the question is not so much whether you succeeded or failed but if you had fun in the process. I wish I had a picture of Keith's face when I ask him that question. I'd put it in the margin for your amusement.

I can go no further without musing over Christ's divinely uncanny ability to waltz right into a life and turn it upside down, inside out, and every which way but loose. Just think how many times those fishermen had prepared and cast their nets together. Picture how many years they had practiced a routine. They weren't fishing for the pure enjoyment of it as my husband does. Fishing was their job. I don't doubt they loved it as most men would, but don't think for a moment it wasn't work. Hard work.

Hear them declare it so. Upon Jesus' suggestion that they "put out into deep water and let down your nets for a catch," Peter answered Jesus, "Master, we've worked hard all night long and caught nothing" (Luke 5:4–5).

Yes, they worked hard. Day in. Day out. Then one day Jesus walked up. And everything changed.

Oh, beloved, isn't that exactly like Him? Jesus walks right up, catches us in the act of being—again today—exactly who we were yesterday, and offers to turn our routine into adventure. Hallelujah! Have you allowed Christ to do that for you? If you're bored with life and stuck in a rut of routine, you may have believed in Christ, but you may not yet have agreed to follow Him. Christ is a lot of things, but boring? Not on your life! Life with Him is indeed a great adventure.

You don't necessarily have to leave behind what you do if He proves your present course to be His will, but I assure you He will have you leave the boredom and routine of it behind. When Jesus Christ takes over our lives, things get exciting!

Consider where you are in this present season of your life. Keep in mind that even our spiritual practices can become very routine. Also keep in mind that living in what we'll call the Great Adventure doesn't mean you don't have challenges or even times of suffering, but it means that you can "see" and take part in the breathtaking work of Christ in your life. What glimpses have you seen of this already? What might be out there waiting for you?

_____

_____

_____

_____

_____

_____

_____

Praying God's Word Today

O Lord, I know that it is only by the abundance of Your faithful love that I have been welcomed into Your house. Therefore, I bow down toward Your holy temple in reverence (Ps. 5:7), amazed at who You are and what You do. You work so that people will be in awe of You, Lord God (Eccles. 3:14). And even if only a few pay attention, may I be one who never grows weary of seeing Your glory in all things, even ordinary things. _____

Day 3

Preparation Day

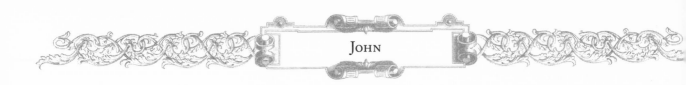
BEFORE YOU BEGIN

Read John 1:35–42

STOP AND CONSIDER

When Jesus turned and noticed them following Him, He asked them, "What are you looking for?" They said to Him, "Rabbi . . . where are You staying?" (v. 38)

At this season of your life, what do you sense you need most: preparation for a fresh work of God? Repair from a tear? Restoration from a fall? _____

_____

_____

How could you demonstrate your willingness to follow Him faithfully into whatever He knows is next for you? _____

_____

_____

_____

Peter, Andrew, James, and John knew Christ at least by reputation based on John the Baptist's faithful ministry, and at least several of them knew Him by a prior encounter. We know from John 1, for example, that two disciples were nearby and heard John the Baptist declare Jesus to be "the Lamb of God" as He passed by (vv. 35–36). Verse 40 identifies one of these men as Andrew. Many scholars believe that John the disciple was the other, since as a rule John did not identify himself in his writings. We know for certain that Peter met Christ as this earlier time because John 1:42 tells us Andrew brought him to meet Jesus.

So when Jesus approached them at their boats, they were primed and readied by God—even if through a short period of time—to leave everything behind and follow Christ anywhere.

In fact, I'd like to suggest that just as James and John were preparing their nets, they themselves had been prepared. The word "preparing" in Mark 1:19 (NIV) can also mean "repairing." The exact same word is used in Galatians 6:1 (NIV) for restoring a fallen brother—"If someone is caught in a sin, you who are spiritual should restore him gently." Oh, how thankful I am that the same God who prepares also repairs and restores.

Joshua 3:5 contains a wonderful challenge: "Consecrate yourselves, because the LORD will do wonders among you tomorrow." God can perform a miracle in any one of us at any time, but amazing things happen when you and I are willing to get prepared for a mighty work of God. Included in that mighty work will most assuredly be what we need most— whether a fresh work, a repair, or a full-scale restoration.

As we get to know John and see events through his eyes, I trust God will be preparing us also. Let's allow God to consecrate us and lay the groundwork for something spectacular. I pray that by the time we reach the end of this book, God will be amazing and astonishing to us. Right this moment, let Jesus look you straight in the eyes and tell you that He knows who you are and who He wants to make you. That's the only way you and I will ever discover the One who calls us and the one we were born to be. Child, a great adventure awaits you.

PRAYING GOD'S WORD TODAY

Father, You have said that if we will purify ourselves from the works of the natural flesh—the sinful inclinations that constantly threaten to trip us up and leave us ineffective—we will be a special instrument in your hand, set apart, useful to the Master, prepared for every good work (2 Tim. 2:21). I offer these on the altar today, Lord, joining those who are fleeing from youthful passions and are instead pursuing righteousness, faith, love, and peace, calling on You from a pure heart (2 Tim. 2:22). _____

_____

_____

_____

_____

_____

_____

_____

_____

_____

_____

_____

_____

_____

_____

_____

_____

DAY 4

A Father's Dilemma

BEFORE YOU BEGIN

Read Mark 1:16–20

STOP AND CONSIDER

Immediately He called them, and they left their father Zebedee
in the boat with the hired men and followed Him. (v. 20)

When have you been called to give up something that you were just beginning to enjoy and appreciate? _____

_____

_____

What have you learned from seasons of separation—those moments when change and transition leave you feeling at a loss? _____

_____

_____

_____

I'm so glad God chose to include the name of James and John's father in Scripture. He wasn't just any man. He wasn't just any father. He was Zebedee. He had a name. He had feelings. He had plans. He was probably close enough to each of his sons' births to hear Salome, his young, inexperienced wife, cry out in pain. He probably wept when he was told he had a son. And then another. No doubt, he praised God for such grace. Daughters were loved, but every man needed a son to carry on the family line, after all.

Two fine sons. That's what Zebedee had. He named them himself. They played in his shadow until they were old enough to work; and if I know anything about teenage boys, they still played plenty behind his back even when they were supposed to be working. Just about the time Zebedee grew exasperated with them, he'd look in their faces and see himself.

At the time when Christ called James and John, I have a feeling they had never been more pleasure or more support. Life is curious. Just about the time you get to reap some of the fruit of your parenting labors, the young, flourishing tree gets transplanted elsewhere.

Keith and I experienced this season of life I'm describing. The summers of our daughters' college years were great fun, and we never secretly wanted to push them back to school or down an aisle. They had never been more delightful, never been easier to care for, and never had more to offer in terms of company and stimulating conversation. I wonder if Zebedee felt the same way about his young adult sons.

Just when Zeb was reaping a harvest of parental rewards, James and John jumped ship. All he had to show for it was a slimy fishing net. What would happen to the business? What about Zebedee and Sons? No matter how Zebedee felt, I have a pretty good feeling God had great compassion on him. After all, He knew how Zebedee felt when John had to be called away from his father's side in order to fulfill his destiny.

Chances are pretty good Zebedee thought their sudden departure was a phase and they'd get over it. Glory to God, they never did. Once we let Jesus Christ really get to us, we never get over Him.

Praying God's Word Today

Father, You inspired John to write of Your love being revealed among us in this way: You sent Your One and Only Son into the world so that we might live through Him (1 John 4:9). So I know, Lord, that You are even more acquainted with loss and separation than I am. May I trust Your heart to know that You are working all things together for the good of those who love You: those who are called according to Your purpose (Rom. 8:28). _____

_____

_____

_____

_____

_____

_____

_____

_____

_____

_____

_____

_____

DAY 5

Time with Jesus

BEFORE YOU BEGIN

Read John 2:1–2, 12

STOP AND CONSIDER

After this, He went down to Capernaum, together with His mother, His brothers, and His disciples, and they stayed there only a few days. (v. 12)

What kinds of benefits begin to flow into your life after spending long periods of time with Christ? How do your attitudes and perspectives begin to change? _____

_____

_____

Perhaps you're still in a fairly broken state right now, not yet fully trusting what you see in Him. What would it take to accept by faith the things He can do if you follow Him?

_____

_____

_____

I love the fact that Jesus talks in words and images His listeners can understand. When He said, "I will make you fishers of men" (Matt. 4:19 NIV), He obviously used terminology Andrew, Peter, James, and John could understand. He didn't use the same terminology with Philip, Nathanael, or Matthew, but I am convinced one part of the sentence applies to every single person Jesus Christ calls. "Come, follow me and *I will make you . . .*" Decades later when God had used these men to change the face of "religion" forever, they still could not boast in themselves. Christ made them the men and the influences they were.

I can't express what these thoughts mean to me. I was such a broken and scattered mess. So emotionally unhealthy. So insecure and full of fear. I am not being falsely modest when I tell you that when Christ called me, He had pitifully little to work with. I was a wreck . . . and stayed that way for longer than I'd like to admit. I have such a long way to go, but this I can say: I followed Christ, and anything that I am or have of value is completely from Him.

So how does Christ "make" a man or a woman? We will explore many ways, but the most immediate way He began building His new followers into the people He wanted them to be was by spending intense time with them and showing them how He worked.

Piecing the Gospels together in a precise chronological order is a task far too challenging for me. I'm relieved to know that it is also a little too challenging for other Bible commentators. What we do know is that Christ and His small and yet incomplete band of followers attended a wedding in Cana together very soon after their union. In fact, John 2:1 says on the third day a wedding took place in Cana in Galilee, but we can't be entirely sure what he meant. It sounds like the third day after John began to follow Jesus.

We are going to explore the wedding more fully when we study the uniqueness of John's Gospel, but for now I'd like you to view the verse immediately following the celebration. John 2:12 (NIV) says, "After this he went down to Capernaum with his mother and brothers and his disciples. There they stayed for a few days."

Christ's family and His disciples obviously enjoyed at least a brief season of peace and harmony. I didn't give that idea any thought until researching for this study. The schism in Christ's family didn't develop until a little while later (John 7:3–5). Eventually we will behold the reconciliation brought by the power of the resurrection. For now, however, picture Christ surrounded by both His family and His new disciples.

What we're studying isn't religious fiction or simple Christian tradition. Christ literally walked into people's lives and transformed them.

I am fairly convinced that we don't really know people until we stay with them for a few days. Can I hear an amen? Although I'm grinning, I have almost always been more blessed than less. Not long ago, Amanda and I got stranded in Tennessee after a conference due to a serious flood in Houston. When I learned the airport was closed, I frantically called Travis, my dear friend and worship leader, and asked if he had room for two more in his van back to Nashville. Without making a single preparation for us, his young family of four graciously received us into their home for two nights. Although we were already very close friends, we bonded for life. The treasure of having part of my ministry family and part of my natural family in fellowship together was priceless.

The disciples were new on the scene. They probably didn't have quite the comfort level interacting with Christ's family for those several days that I enjoyed with my worship leader's family. Still, they got to see Christ interact with His own family—an opportunity that I think was critical. Soon they would see Him perform all manner of miracles. They already had witnessed the changing of water to wine, but the sights they would soon see would nearly take their breath away. You see, people are much harder to change than water.

As they watched this man named Jesus—this carpenter's son—as they fellowshiped with Him then witnessed His work, what do you think they saw? Consistency? Versatility? Unwavering passion? Or a lamb as often as a lion? The center of all attention? Or a teacher that became a student of all those around Him? We know they saw absolute authenticity, but how do you imagine they saw it portrayed?

Don't think for a minute that thinking about such matters is a waste of time. The more we grasp the flesh-and-blood reality of these encounters and try to imagine the intimate details the disciples witnessed in Christ the better! What we're studying isn't religious fiction or simple Christian tradition. Christ walked into people's lives and transformed them. You and I want nothing less.

Let your imagination run awhile. What do you suppose were some of the things that these early followers immediately saw in Jesus? What do you think caught their eye and fastened them to His leadership?

_____

_____

_____

_____

_____

_____

_____

_____

_____

PRAYING GOD'S WORD TODAY

Lord Jesus, Your prophet declared that You had no form or splendor that we should look at You, no appearance that we should desire You. You were despised and rejected by men, a man of suffering who knew what sickness was. You were like one people turned away from; You were despised, and we didn't value You (Isa. 53:2–3). Yet some did. And as I spend time with You today, I want to be like those early disciples who saw something about You that caused grown men to walk away from established lives and keep following You to the death. You are beautiful, Lord, to me. _____

DAY 6

A Sheer Show
of Strength

BEFORE YOU BEGIN
Read Mark 1:21–28

STOP AND CONSIDER

They were all amazed . . . saying, "What is this? A new teaching with authority!
He commands even the unclean spirits, and they obey Him." (v. 27)

Why does God often seem to delight new converts with bold, visible displays of His glory, while trusting His older saints to follow with less flowery fireworks? _____

_____

_____

How dependent have you been on big splashes of emotion and spiritual splendor? What tends to happen to your Christian fervor when things are quieter and more at ease? _____

_____

_____

_____

The disciples saw Christ perform some eye-opening miracles almost from the start. Although we are saving further comments on the wedding at Cana for later, we know that it was the location of Christ's first miracle and that John's reference to the time frame of the wedding was "the third day" (John 2:1). The next occurrence in sequence was Christ's trip to Capernaum with His mother, brothers, and disciples (John 2:12). The events we will study next probably happened during the same stay in Capernaum, so imagine them falling next in sequence.

Jesus had just called Andrew, Peter, James, and John. Mark tells us they went to Capernaum (Mark 1:21). Picture these four fishermen mingling in the crowd gathered that Sabbath in the synagogue. I have an idea Christ's new disciples didn't just watch Jesus as He preached. I have a feeling they watched the reaction of others who were listening to Him as well. Mind you, at least Peter and Andrew lived in Capernaum at that time (v. 29). A town this size had only one Jewish synagogue, so they worshiped with virtually the same people week after week. They knew them personally. Some were relatives. Others were neighbors or business associates. Imagine the kinds of reactions the disciples saw on these familiar faces as Jesus preached.

Talk about an interesting service! If an "amazing" message were not enough excitement, just then a man in their synagogue who was possessed by an evil spirit cried out, "What do You have to do with us, Jesus—Nazarene? Have You come to destroy us? I know who You are—the Holy One of God!" (v. 24). Suddenly their heads turned toward the opponent, almost like spectators in a tennis match.

I wonder if the crowd knew this man had an evil spirit before this moment or if they had been oblivious for years to the nature of his problems. Had they known, I'm not sure they would have allowed him in the synagogue, so my feeling is that the man may have kept it covered to some extent. Goodness knows Satan loves a good disguise. Somehow, however, when the authority of Christ was released in that place, the demons lost their cover. Jesus has a way of bringing the devil right out of some people, doesn't He?

Yes, the mere presence of Jesus had caused the man—or should we say the demon?—to cry out at the appearance of divine authority. Jesus commanded the demons to come out of the man, but He also added something more. He commanded the spirit to be quiet.

John and the other disciples would see many miracles, but Jesus was after something more. He was out to build maturity into this group.

Picture John witnessing these events. Many scholars believe he was the youngest of the disciples. One strong basis for this deduction is his positioning and apparent role at the Passover meal just before Jesus' crucifixion. We'll examine those events later, but for now keep in mind that the youngest at the Passover meal usually sat nearest the father or father figure so he could ask the traditional questions. I will refrain from building any doctrines on this deduction (since I could obviously be off base), but I am personally convinced enough that John was the youngest that I'll adopt this philosophy. If he was, can you imagine his face in particular while Jesus encountered—then cast out—these demons?

I think he probably experienced an entire concoction of emotions. Young men dearly love competitions, so he must have savored seeing his new team "win," even if only one Player was involved in the match. I have to think the encounter also scared him half to death. One thing that might have offset his fear was that he had to be indescribably impressed with his new mentor.

He wasn't the only one. Mark 1:21 tells us the crowds were generally amazed and astonished by Christ's teachings, but Mark 1:27 intensifies the adjectives by saying they were "all amazed" by His demonstration of authority over the demons.

We do love a show, don't we? When I think how patient Christ has been with our human preference for divine fireworks, I am more amazed than ever. Christ knows us intimately. He knows how to get our attention, but He also desires that we grow up and seek His presence and glory more than the display of His might. John and the other disciples would see many miracles, but Jesus was after something more. He was out to build maturity into this group.

I have a feeling by the time the fishermen reached Capernaum with Jesus, something more tagged along—the news of their leaving Zebedee holding the net. I don't doubt for a minute that these young men whose reputations were on the line reveled in the grand reaction people in the community had to their new Leader. What could be more exciting than being associated with the most powerful and popular new man on the scene?

What kinds of temptations come along with being on God's "side"? What elements of our human nature must be watched like a hawk when we begin championing the way of Christ among our unsaved family, friends, and others? _____

_____

_____

_____

_____

_____

_____

_____

_____

Praying God's Word Today

It is quite obvious, God, that I have not yet reached the goal or am already fully mature, but I make every effort to take hold of this life You have given me, because it is You, Lord Jesus, who have taken hold of me. So may I forget what is behind, reach forward to what is ahead, and pursue as my goal the prize promised by Your heavenly call (Phil. 3:12–14). Help me to be drawn to You and You alone, Lord, not just to what You do. _____

DAY 7

Scenes on
a Sabbath Day

BEFORE YOU BEGIN

Read Mark 1:29–34

STOP AND CONSIDER

Simon's mother-in-law was lying in bed with a fever, and they told Him about her at once. So He went to her, took her by the hand, and raised her up. (vv. 30–31)

John was a human being just like you. How do you suppose the sights and sounds of Jesus' first miracles impacted him and the other followers of Christ? _____

_____

_____

Think about the last time you encountered someone who was suffering terribly. What kinds of feelings did you have in response to their suffering? _____

_____

_____

_____

Think of events such as Jesus' birth, baptism, crucifixion, and resurrection as primary events that can indeed be placed in time sequence. Then consider the specific incidents from Jesus' life as secondary events. We won't often be able to put the secondary events of the four Gospels into an unquestionable chronological order. Each of the Gospel writers selected the events and stories for specific reasons. Matthew wrote to show that Jesus is the Jewish Messiah. Mark wrote to tell the Romans about what Jesus did. Luke wrote to show that Jesus came to be the Savior for all peoples, and John wrote to show the meaning of Jesus' ministry. The Spirit led them to write to convey the message, not to tell us the order of events.

Based on identical time sequencing in Mark and Luke and with nothing in Matthew or John to refute it, however, I believe we can rightly assume that the first healing of the sick ever witnessed by the disciples was in Simon Peter's home.

Before we talk about the healing, however, let's consider a bit about the order of events in the Gospels. Surely an early turning point came in the hearts and minds of the disciples when healing hit home. I know it did for me. Seeing Him work in a church service is one thing. Witnessing His healing in the life of your own family is another. That's when a person begins to get it through her head that Jesus doesn't just love church. He loves people.

By comparing Mark 1:21 and 29, we see it was the Sabbath day. Jesus had delivered the demon-possessed man in the synagogue. "As soon as they left the synagogue, they went into Simon and Andrew's house with James and John" (v. 29). Christ raised the ire of the Pharisees on more than a few occasions by picking this particular day of the week for healings. It seems as if He were making a point. Later we're going to see that in many ways this was the perfect day of the week for healing.

I didn't realize until doing some research that even His first healing was on the Sabbath. Obviously, Christ saw the purpose of the day far differently than many of His contemporaries. Apparently Simon Peter's mother-in-law was healed just in time to rise from the bed and get ready for company. As soon as the sun set, the whole town gathered at her door. They brought Jesus the sick and demon possessed for healing.

Have you ever seen someone receive an instantaneous physical healing like those described in this text? I've known plenty of people God healed physically, but I haven't had many chances to watch the manifestation of an instant healing take place before my very eyes. Few of us choose to confront the suffering around us because we feel so helpless. Imagine the contrast between the agony of seeing human suffering and the ecstasy of seeing them healed. What would such an experience have been like for Mother Teresa, for instance, as she daily died to her own desire for personal comfort and confronted the unimaginable suffering in Calcutta? Then to see many healed? Somehow my mind can hardly even fathom the range of emotions.

> Few of us choose to confront the suffering around us because we feel so helpless. Imagine instead the ecstasy of seeing them healed.

John had observed hundreds of Sabbaths in his life. Imagine that he awakened on the morning prior to these miraculous events with a fresh wave of, "I can hardly believe what I've done! I wonder what my mom and dad are thinking right now." He must have been excited and unsure, and his soul was filled with the reality that something new was looming on the horizon.

He prepared to go to the synagogue for services just as he had done all his life, only this time he got a bit more than he bargained for. The scroll was unraveled, and the Scripture for the day's service was read. Then Jesus took the role of rabbi, sat down, and preached the curly locks nearly off their heads.

Just then a man possessed by demons started shouting, and John saw Jesus get stern, perhaps for the first time. In an astounding show of power, Jesus cast out the demons, causing the man to shake violently. John thought as long as he lived, he would never forget the sound of those demons shrieking. He and the other disciples then walked together to Simon Peter's house, whispering all the way about what they'd seen. Simon Peter's mother-in-law was sick with a fever, so Jesus took her by the hand, helped her up, and the fever left her so instantaneously she began to serve them. Then they began to hear sounds at the door. Murmurings. Shrieking. Crying. Sounds of moaning. Sounds of hope. What's that—hope? Yes, hope—hope which says, "What He did for her, He might do for me." And that He did.

When John had awakened that morning, his mind could not have conceived just how many mercies were new that particular sunrise. I can only imagine the kinds of things that went through the mind of the young disciple the following night. He probably tossed and turned, unable to clear his head and rest. Perhaps he and James whispered from their pallets until they were overtaken by exhaustion and finally fell asleep.

What would the world think if they could see the compassion that's on display in Jesus' treatment of people in this scene from Scripture? Assuming they may not be reading it any time soon, how could we help them see it in some other way? _____

_____

_____

_____

_____

_____

_____

PRAYING GOD'S WORD TODAY

It's only because of Your faithful love and mercy, O Lord, that we do not perish, for Your mercies never end. They are new every morning, just as they were new on that Sabbath morning so many centuries ago. How great is Your faithfulness, Lord God of glory! You are my portion, says my soul, therefore I put all my hope in You (Lam. 3:22–24). _____

DAY 8

Good for What

Ails You

Before You Begin
Read Matthew 4:23–25

Stop and Consider

They brought to Him all those who were afflicted, those suffering from various diseases and intense pains, the demon-possessed, the epileptics, and the paralytics. (v. 24)

Perhaps it would take other words than these to articulate the depth and specifics of your need. Take this space to list what you're going through and where you're hurting. _____

_____

_____

_____

Now think of others you know who are suffering physically, emotionally, or relationally right now. What kinds of need are all around you today? _____

_____

_____

_____

As I imagine all that happened that Saturday and all they saw, I know one of the thoughts I'd have had if I had been John. *Is there anything the man can't do?* He watched Jesus practically bring the house down with His teaching. He watched Him confront and cast out a demon. He watched Him not only heal Simon's mother-in-law but instantly restore her strength. Then every manner of distress landed on their doorstep.

I love Matthew Henry's words of commentary on the scene at the door. "How powerful the Physician was; he healed all that were brought to him, though ever so many. Nor was it some one particular disease, that Christ set up for the cure of, but he healed those that were sick of divers [various, diverse] diseases, for his word was a panpharmacon—a salve for every sore."[3]

His Word was a "panpharmacon." Ah, yes. I have yet to have an ailment God had no salve to soothe. What may be even more peculiar is that I have yet to have an ailment of soul that God's Word was not the first to point out, diagnose, then heal. His Word is far more glorious, powerful, and fully applicable than we have any idea. You very likely did not pick up this particular devotional book because you sought healing. You would surely have picked other titles. But based on my own experience and many references in Scripture, you will undoubtedly receive some fresh diagnoses and, if you cooperate, a new measure of healing. As will I. I'm counting on it.

That's the nature of His Word. As Psalm 107:20 says, "He sent His word and healed them; He rescued them from the Pit." How often God has had to send forth His Word and begin the healing to get me healthy enough to face the diagnosis!

I want you to revel in something wonderful. Every time God has prepared us with His Word and gotten us to a point that we can receive a hard "pill" to swallow from Him, healing has already begun. Once He confronts us, we never need to be overwhelmed by how far we have to go. If we've heard Him through His Word, healing has already begun.

Take heart. He is the Panpharmacon.

PRAYING GOD'S WORD TODAY

Lord, the moonlight will be as bright as the sunlight, and the sunlight will be seven times brighter—like the light of seven days—on the day that You bandage Your people's injuries and heal the wounds we have endured (Isa. 30:26). Whether here on this fallen Earth or in the splendor of a new one, I know I will see the sun of righteousness rising with healing in its wings, and we will go out and playfully jump like calves from the stall (Mal. 4:2).

DAY 9

Ambush at Dawn

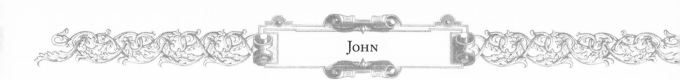
BEFORE YOU BEGIN

Read Mark 1:35–39

STOP AND CONSIDER

Simon and his companions went searching for Him.

They found Him and said, "Everyone's looking for You!" (vv. 36–37)

Notice that these "companions" of Jesus had not been called disciples yet. What do you think was still missing from their carton of character traits before they could legitimately be known as learners and pupils of the Messiah? _____

_____

_____

What keeps any of us from putting higher value on the times we spend with the Lord in solitary places? _____

_____

_____

_____

Ah, here we have an insight into the present state of mind of Jesus' first followers. Forget what Jesus did in private! They wanted to be seen in public with the popular Jesus! We're not going to be too hard on them, now, because they were demonstrating a normal part of adolescent Christianity. We're the same way in our spiritual immaturity. At first we are far more excited about corporate worship than we are private worship.

The terminology of the original language tells us they were tracking Jesus down, almost like a manhunt. The Greek word translated "to look," is often used in a hostile sense.[4] I'm not suggesting they were hostile toward Jesus but that they were quite anxious and maybe even a little put out with Him that He wasn't where all the people were. We see no indication from the text that they hesitated for a moment of respect or awe when they found Jesus praying. They barreled on the scene with, "Everyone is looking for you!"

I would like to offer a little conjecture that the companions tracking down Jesus may have been Peter, James, and John. Later in His ministry, these three men were chosen by Christ to watch Him on several different occasions in the inner places. Something caused Jesus to single them out, and it wasn't their spiritual maturity. I think two primary motivations compelled Christ to draw the three into several intimate places:

• The fact that they just didn't "get it" at times.
• The fact that Jesus knew once they did "get it," they'd really get it!

In other words, I wonder if Christ might have thought, "So you're not the boundaries types, are you? Okay, I'll take you behind some ordinary boundaries, but I'll hold you responsible for what you learn while you're there." Just food for thought.

I have a friend whose little boy thought he was the teacher's pet because she seated him in class right in front of her desk. He didn't realize for years that she was motivated by his discipline problems. Why didn't she just send him to the principal instead of expending so much energy on him? Because she knew the child had a student in him, and she was determined to find it. And she did. We're going to see Peter, James, and John get their desks moved to the front of the class. Just like children, they might be tempted at times to think the Rabbi moved them there because they were the Teacher's pets.

PRAYING GOD'S WORD TODAY

Dear Lord Jesus, I echo Your words to the Father as I approach Your throne today: "I know that You always hear Me" (John 11:42). And as I rise up to leave from this place, may I say with You again, "Father, I thank You that You heard Me" (John 11:41). What a privilege to be welcomed into Your presence. I never want to tread here lightly.

DAY 10

Behind the Veil

BEFORE YOU BEGIN

Read Mark 5:35–43

STOP AND CONSIDER

He took the child by the hand and said to her, *"Talitha koum!"* (which is translated, "Little girl, I say to you, get up!"). . . . At this they were utterly astounded. (vv. 41–42)

Being in the same room with death has a riveting effect on anyone. What do you think Jesus had in mind by asking Peter, James, and John here to witness this moment? _____

_____

_____

Is there anything you've given up for dead in your life, assuming it was beyond Christ's power to reverse or transform? How could He bring life into this very situation? _____

_____

_____

_____

I want to remind you of our objective. You may otherwise be frustrated over my leap-frogging from place to place in Scripture. Although I wish we could go through every step the disciples took with Christ, the purpose of this journey is to draw riches from the life and letters of John. We've taken the first steps of his encounters with Jesus rather slowly because he was among those first chosen to follow Christ. For a time we will pick up the pace rather dramatically as we leapfrog from scene to scene. As we focus on the synoptic Gospels, our objective is to concentrate on the settings where John is named or known to be present.

Keep in mind that Jesus had many followers, but He chose twelve from the many to walk nearest to Him. Every moment the twelve spent with Jesus was significant, but over the next couple of days we're going to look at two scenes with some common denominators that no doubt had a profound effect on John. Try your best to view each occurrence from his point of view. Keep in mind that John was probably the youngest of the apostles and younger brother to one. Think of him as flesh and blood, and imagine what each experience might have been like for him.

We find scene one in this passage from Mark, chapter 5. The synagogue ruler named Jairus had requested that Jesus heal his daughter, and they were on the way to his home. Men met them and told Jairus not to bother the Rabbi because the girl had already died. Jesus told Jairus, "Don't be afraid. Only believe" (v. 36).

I am fascinated by what Jesus did next. First, "He did not let anyone accompany Him except Peter, James, and John, James' brother" (v. 37). This reduced number proceeded to the home. The mourners had already gathered. In fact, they laughed when Jesus said the girl was not dead. So He drove the crowd out of the house. He took the three disciples and the girl's parents into the room with Him. Jesus then raised the girl from the dead with a mere verbal command.

I can't help wondering what went through the minds of the three men when they were allowed to follow Jesus to a place the others weren't invited. I know what would have gone through my feminine mind. Women tend to be so relational. I hardly would have

been able to enjoy the privilege without fretting over the others being left out. Then, of course, I would have worried about whether they would be mad at me when we got back. I would imagine for days that they were acting a little weird. In fact, knowing I would have fretted myself half to death, Jesus most likely wouldn't have bothered letting me come. No telling how many things I've missed because I make a knot out of the simplest string.

Oh, but how I would have hated to miss the eyeful the three got that particular day. Raising the stone-cold dead is nothing less than divine. This scene was not business as usual no matter how many miracles the three had seen and even performed.

I have been with several people right around their times of death, and I was utterly amazed each time how quickly the body grew cold. In spiritual terms, the soul is what keeps a body warm. Physical death occurs when the soul (meaning the immaterial part of a person—soul and spirit) departs the body. At its exodus, the warmth of life departs as well. We can be comforted by the fresh realization that the spiritual life is in the soul, and the soul continues living. We talk about the finality of death, but it has relatively little finality to the believer.

> He's not very likely to raise our loved one from the dead, but He can do countless other things to get us through our losses.

I'm so glad Jesus didn't listen to those who discouraged Jairus from "bothering" the teacher any more. Their reason was because the girl was dead. But the death of a loved one is no time to quit "bothering" Jesus. No, He's not very likely to raise our loved one from the dead, but He can do countless other things to get us through our losses. Comfort is the most obvious need, but we have others.

I often talk to people who remain hamstrung by a death that has left many issues or answers unresolved. If I may be so bold, sometimes the missing person is not a loved one but an unforgiven or unforgiving one with whom we needed to make peace. Hopelessness

often ensues. Depression can result. Sometimes we are convinced that all parties must be alive and kicking for us to gain peace in a situation.

Needless to say, the ideal time to make peace with others is while everyone's still breathing. But if it's too late, bother the Teacher! He doesn't have our limitations or rationalizations. Has a death left you with unfinished business? Finish it with Jesus.

Among other things, this is a lesson in keeping our relationships honest and authentic—our love expressed, our vows kept, our forgiveness current. Is there anything in your life right now that another's death could leave unresolved? _____

_____

_____

_____

_____

_____

_____

_____

_____

Praying God's Word Today

Lord, just as You showed Your disciples, You are the One who destroys the burial shroud—the oppressive weight it presses down upon us—the shroud over all the peoples, the sheet that covers all the nations. You, in fact, have destroyed death forever. And You will one day wipe away the tears from every face and remove death's disgrace from the whole earth, for You have spoken it, Lord God (Isa. 25:7–8). You give us freedom from everything that threatens to keep us in bondage, from everything that threatens to keep us from You.

DAY 11

Triple Wow

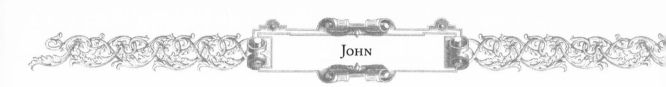
BEFORE YOU BEGIN

Read Mark 9:2–10

STOP AND CONSIDER

His clothes became dazzling—extremely white as no launderer on earth could whiten them. Elijah appeared to them with Moses, and they were talking with Jesus. (vv. 3–4)

Where has God taken you personally to transfigure your perception of Him? What scenes, images, and memories attest to His total "otherness"—to His transcendence of man?

_____

_____

What could you do or practice more often to keep yourself reminded that, although He is near, He is far, far beyond us? _____

_____

_____

_____

Although much time elapsed and many significant events occurred between the healing of Jairus's daughter and the transfiguration, what makes these two scenes priorities at this point in the book is the inclusion of only three disciples.

In Mark 5:37, the three were listed as "Peter, James, and John, James' brother." In this scene, John is no longer named like a tagalong brother. At this point, we see his identity in Scripture undoubtedly emerging. Also note that Jesus didn't just let Peter, James, and John come along. He *took* them. He "led them" there (Mark 9:2).

God's will always expresses divine intention. Just as Jesus was intentional toward the experiences and exposures of the three, Christ is intentional toward us. He never bosses us or appoints us to something for the sheer sake of presuming authority. His will always has purpose. Sometimes we go our own ways, and God still has mercy on us and shows us something there. Other times we beg Him to allow us to go a certain place and He consents. Still other times God takes us places we never intended to go. Those are places where He will reveal Himself to us in ways we didn't even know He existed.

All three synoptic Gospels record the transfiguration. Matthew's Gospel supplies the detail that the three disciples fell facedown to the ground. I am convinced that the people of God miss many appropriate opportunities to fall facedown to the ground, not in an emotional frenzy but in complete awe of God. We don't have a clue who we're dealing with. I believe one of Jesus' chief reasons for transfiguring Himself before the three disciples was to say, "I am not like you. This is just a glimpse of who I am."

Remember, Jesus had equipped them with supernatural power to perform some of the same miracles He performed. What would keep these three from thinking that just maybe, in time, they might be His peers? God forbid the thought! Jesus is not a superhuman. He is God—the beloved, divine Son of Him who occupies the throne of all creation.

God says in Psalm 50:21, "You thought I was just like you. But I will rebuke you and lay out the case before you." One primary reason He takes us to places we've never been is to show us He's not like anyone else.

Praying God's Word Today

Thinking of You transfigured before Peter, James, and John, what else can I do today but join them in facedown awe and reverence, worshiping you as the image of the invisible God, the firstborn over all creation (Col. 1:15)—the radiance of His glory, the exact expression of His nature, sustaining all things by Your powerful word (Heb. 1:3). Praise You, Lord, now and forever. Praise You—praise You, Lord.

DAY 12

High Horses

BEFORE YOU BEGIN

Read Luke 9:46–56

STOP AND CONSIDER

When the disciples James and John saw this, they said, "Lord, do You want us to call down fire from heaven to consume them?" But He turned and rebuked them. (vv. 54–55)

Strange, isn't it, that we can begin to take pride in the fact that God has humbled Himself to draw near us. When do you feel this rising in you the most? _____

_____

_____

How has God chosen to deal with this feeling in you? And what is different about you when humility starts taking its place? _____

_____

_____

_____

We last saw John, his brother, and his buddy Peter as they viewed sights the others could hardly have imagined. They beheld revelations of His glory both in raising the dead and conferring with those long supposed dead. One might say you'd have to be dead to be unaffected by such sights, but obviously in both cases the dead were highly affected! No one remained unchanged. But how were the disciples changing? That's the question.

In this passage from Luke 9, we see the disciples arguing about which of them would be greatest, then we see John—not once but twice—snapping the suspenders of his perceived superiority, bringing a sense of entitlement to the inner circle.

I'm sitting here shaking my head. Oh, not just at *them*. At myself. At the whole lot of us. Sometimes I wonder why God doesn't give up on us when we cop attitudes like these. I am so grateful that God is both nearsighted and farsighted. He sees us as we really are, and He sees how we'll really be. I'm pretty convinced that only the latter keeps the former alive.

Perhaps John's age didn't help. Life simply hadn't had time to beat him over the head with humility—not like Moses, who had all of forty years on the far side of the desert followed by a flock of aggravating people to humble the exclusivity right out of him.

In a wonderfully peculiar account in Numbers 11:24–30, Moses faced a similar situation. He took the elders of Israel into the tent of meeting. There the Spirit of God came upon them and they prophesied. Two of the elders, however, did not come with the group. Yet these two also began to prophesy in the camp. When Joshua heard what was happening, he asked almost the exact question as John in our incident above. He asked if he should stop the two. Moses responded, "Are you jealous on my account? If only all the LORD's people were prophets, and the LORD would place His Spirit on them" (Num. 11:29).

I'll never forget standing in the resource room of my office with a friend who asked, "What does it feel like to look at all these books with your name on them?" My face screwed up into a knot, and I said, "All they represent to me is one holy beatin' after another!" I am sad to say that much of what I've learned has come with the rod of God, but things are beginning to change, aren't they, Father? I hope so.

PRAYING GOD'S WORD TODAY

Lord, as You daily enlighten the eyes of my heart to know the hope of Your calling and the glorious riches of Your inheritance among the saints (Eph. 1:18), may I not exalt myself but only You, Lord. For it is the immeasurable greatness of *Your* power, Lord Jesus, that has been given to us who believe, and all of it is according to the working of *Your* vast strength (Eph. 1:19), not from any effort of our own.

DAY 13

Growing Uppity

BEFORE YOU BEGIN

Read Mark 10:35–45

STOP AND CONSIDER

Whoever wants to become great among you must be your servant,

and whoever wants to be first among you must be a slave to all. (vv. 43–44)

Being very honest, where are the most telling pockets of immaturity in your life? In what areas does this "servant" and "slave" mentality have the hardest time getting through?

_____

_____

Thinking of some of the most mature believers you know, what is it that sets them apart?

_____

_____

_____

_____

James and John painted a pretty good picture of spiritual toddlerhood, didn't they? But let's face it. All of us have to go through spiritual toddlerhood and adolescence to get to a place of maturity. We don't ordinarily leap up. We grow up.

For a few moments, however, James and John did nothing but descend deeper and deeper into the quicksand of their own self-absorption. (And never doubt it is quicksand.) In this scene, James and John made only three statements: "Teacher, we want You to do something for us if we ask You" (v. 35), "Allow us to sit at Your right and at Your left in Your glory" (v. 37), and a third statement from verse 39 that we'll consider in a moment. Meditate on these. Try to capture the emotions and attitudes behind them. Do you see a growing audacity with each statement?

And don't think for a minute they wouldn't have dug themselves deeper if given the opportunity. Had Christ told them He might consider one on His right and one on His left, how long do you think it would have taken them to rumble over who would sit where?

Their famous last words almost slay me. After Christ asked, "Are you able to drink the cup I drink or to be baptized with the baptism I am baptized with?" they answered without hesitation: "We are able." They didn't have any idea what they were talking about because they didn't have any idea what Christ was talking about. Soon they would. One day in the distant future they would sip from the cup and know the baptism of His suffering. But in their present state they needed a baby bottle, not a cup.

Our problem is often the same as theirs. We let the human image of Christ mislead us into downsizing Him. "If He'd just stoop a little and we stood on our tiptoes, we'd be just about side by side. One at His left. One at His right." But I am convinced that if we, present company included, really "got" the concept of being chosen and called by the divine Son of God, His Spirit would have to set us on our feet for us to get off our faces (Ezek. 2:1). Yes, we've been chosen and, yes, we've been called, and we'll know we're grasping the concept when our humanity is cloaked in humility—not "Teacher, we want You to do something for us," but "Teach us to do for You whatever You ask."

Praying God's Word Today

Lord God, I know well what it's like to be haughty in mind and spirit, to be known by You from afar (Ps. 138:6) when I could instead be living within the full experience of Your pleasure, adorned with Your salvation, celebrating and shouting for joy in Your presence (Ps. 149:4–5), enjoying all the benefits of nearness. Because of Your name, Lord, forgive my sin, for it is great (Ps. 25:11). Humble me that I may eat and be satisfied, seeking You, Lord, forever (Ps. 22:26).

DAY 14

Secret Missions

Before You Begin

Read Luke 22:7–13

Stop and Consider

Jesus sent Peter and John, saying, "Go and prepare
the Passover meal for us, so we can eat it." (v. 8)

How deeply do you believe that each day is another opportunity to be on mission with God, that He has tasks in mind for you today that are specifically ordained for your life?

_____

_____

How does your response to the above question affect the way you approach your morning, your lunch hour, your free time at home or around town? _____

_____

_____

_____

Christ's appointments are never haphazard. He can accomplish anything He desires by merely thinking it into existence. That He assigns men and women to certain tasks implies that the experience of the servant or beneficiary is often as important as the accomplishment. Sometimes more so. God can do anything He wants. He sovereignly chooses to employ mortals to flesh out an invisible work in the visible realm . . . even Jesus the perfect Word made flesh.

I believe that Peter and John were not only chosen for the job of preparing the Passover but that the job was chosen for them. When I considered this scene in *Jesus the One and Only*, I shared what I believe is far more than a coincidence: Peter and John's repetitive references in their letters to Christ as the Lamb. They seemed to have understood the concept of the Paschal Lamb like none of the other writers of the New Testament. I believe a tremendous part of their understanding came in retrospect after their preparation for the last Passover with Christ.

But God added another fresh insight to this as I became more deeply aware of the early influence John the Baptist had upon Peter and John. We know that each was either directly discipled by the Baptizer or indirectly influenced through their brothers. John 1:29 tells us that these disciples first encountered Jesus through the words of the Baptizer: "Look, the Lamb of God, who takes away the sin of the world!"

Jesus would not rest until He taught Peter and John exactly what that title meant. The pair didn't run by the Old City market and grab a saran-wrapped package of trimmed lamb for a buck fifty a pound. No, they picked out a live lamb and then had the sweet thing slaughtered. Very likely they held it still for the knife. Most of us can hardly imagine all that was involved in preparing for a Passover, but you can be sure that none of it was wasted.

That's one of the things I love about Christ. He's not into waste management. If He gives us a task or assigns us to a difficult season, every ounce of our experience is meant for our instruction and completion if only we'll let Him finish the work.

The other day I came across a verse that causes me to stop, meditate, and ask big things from God every time I see it. Psalm 25:14 (NIV) says, "The LORD confides in those who fear him; he makes his covenant known to them." I desperately want God to be able to confide in me, don't you? The King James Version puts it this way: "The secret of the LORD is with them that fear him." I want God to tell me His secrets! I believe these hidden treasures are not secret because He tells them only to a chosen few, but because not many seek to know Him and tarry with Him long enough to find out.

I truly believe that if we're willing to see, God uses every difficulty and every assignment to confide deep things to us.

I believe as Peter and John prepared the Passover meal that day, they were privy to many secrets that became clearer and clearer to them as time passed. Ecclesiastes 3:11 says that God makes everything beautiful in its time. I truly believe that if we're willing to see, God uses every difficulty and every assignment to confide deep things to us, and that the lessons are not complete until their beauty has been revealed. I fear, however, that we have such an attention deficit that we settle for bearable when beauty was just around the corner.

Surely many years and Passover celebrations passed before Peter and John fully assimilated the profound significance of the one in which Jesus became the Lamb. John never could get over it. From the pen of an elderly, shaking hand, we find over twenty references to the Lamb in the Book of Revelation. And it was Peter, his sidekick, who wrote:

> For you know that you were redeemed from your empty way of life inherited from the fathers, not with perishable things, like silver or gold, but with the precious blood of Christ, like that of a lamb without defect or blemish. (1 Pet. 1:18–19)

Look at that opening expression of 1 Peter 1:18 again: "from your empty way of life inherited from the fathers." When I think of a Jewish heritage, I imagine it to be anything but empty! We Americans are such a hodgepodge of cultures that many of us lack the rich traditions of other less alloyed cultures. And who could have enjoyed richer ways of life and more tradition than those handed down by Jewish forefathers to their sons and daughters? Yet Peter called them empty. Why?

I think because once He saw their fulfillment in Jesus Christ, he knew that these "inheritances" were empty without Him. Once he knew the true Passover Lamb, an Old Testament Passover meant nothing without its fulfillment in Jesus. Christ became everything, and all former things were empty without Him.

Think of one or two particular situations that are present in your life right now. What "secrets" of God's will and way are you learning as you go through these seasons of time?

_____

_____

_____

_____

_____

_____

_____

PRAYING GOD'S WORD TODAY

Father, it gives me great encouragement to know that You are a friend to the upright, that You take us into Your confidence (Prov. 3:32). And that because of being rightly related with You through Jesus Christ, we can understand Your teaching if we truly want to know Your will (John 7:17).

DAY 15

Lean In

BEFORE YOU BEGIN
Read John 13:21–30

STOP AND CONSIDER

One of His disciples, the one Jesus loved, was reclining close beside Jesus.
Simon Peter motioned to him to find out who it was He was talking about. (vv. 23–24)

What kind of person is most likely to be "close" to Jesus? Does it require a certain temperament or disposition—a particular kind of upbringing or background? _____

_____

_____

What are the best parts about being close to Him on a regular, ongoing basis? What do you miss most when you're not? _____

_____

_____

_____

John's location at the Passover meal constitutes one of the chief reasons many scholars believe John was the youngest disciple. At the traditional Jewish Passover, the youngest child at the table who is able to talk often sits nearest the father or father figure and asks the traditional questions that prompt the father to tell the story of deliverance from Egypt. The room was small enough for Peter to ask Jesus a question even if he was seated at the opposite end of the table. The fact that he prompted John to ask the question suggests that John may have assumed the role as the official petitioner that evening.

I also love imagining that the youngest among them might have had the least protocol and acted as he felt, not just according to what was proper. Hence his leaning against Jesus. Glory! You see, there's just nothing doctrinal about John's leaning on Jesus. It wasn't the law. It wasn't in the proverbial Passover book of rules. John didn't have to lean on Jesus to talk to Him. Christ could hear him just fine. John leaned on Him because he wanted to. Because he loved Him. Because He was . . . leanable. Approachable. Downright lovable.

Both of my daughters are very affectionate, but my older is without a doubt more proper. My youngest wouldn't know the word "protocol" if it were tattooed on her forehead. (I hope I don't give her any ideas. She's threatened a tattoo before.) From the clues we gather here and there, I like to think that John was somehow the same way with Jesus. Very likely, he was the baby of this family. And his affection for Jesus wasn't encumbered by silly things like protocol. I love that about him.

One of our primary tasks through this journey is to explore the deep affection that flowed like a teeming brook between Jesus and John. I'll just be honest with you. I want what they had. I want what God and David had. I want what Christ and Paul had. If a mortal can experience it with the Immortal Invisible, I want it. I want to know this love that surpasses knowledge so that I may be filled to the measure of all the fullness of God (Eph. 3:19). All else is just an empty way of life handed down by bored and unmotivated forefathers. No thanks. Give me Jesus. If I make someone else uncomfortable, well . . . that's just too bad.

Praying God's Word Today

I gaze on You in the sanctuary to see Your strength and Your glory (Ps. 63:2). And when on my bed, I think of You. I meditate on You during the night watches because You are my help; I will rejoice in the shadow of Your wings. I follow close to You; Your right hand holds on to me (Ps. 63:6–8). In public, in private, my desire is to be close to You.

DAY 16

The Judas in Us

BEFORE YOU BEGIN
Read Luke 22:1–6

STOP AND CONSIDER

The chief priests and the scribes were looking for a way to put Him to death. . . . Then Satan entered Judas, called Iscariot, who was numbered among the Twelve. (vv. 2–3)

We want to believe the best in people. But at times we need to be discerning enough to say, "Something's wrong." What does the church need to do in situations like these? _____

_____

_____

How are you protecting your heart and feet from walking the betrayer's path? What can you do to help others keep their lives open and honest before the Lord? _____

_____

_____

_____

Few things startle and shake us to the core like the sudden revelation of a Judas. Maybe because we can't believe we didn't see it coming. Maybe because we're terrified that if one of us could be Judas, couldn't we all? We are terrified by our similarities! And rightly we should be. But one thing sets us apart. Judas sold his soul to the devil.

John 13:28 tells us no one at the meal understood. But over the course of years and countless replays of the scene in the mind of the apostle John, he knew the devil entered into Judas at that table right before their very eyes. How did he know?

Christ taught in John 14:26 that the Holy Spirit is also the Holy Reminder. He can reveal the truth even in something past and remind us what He was teaching us, though we were unable to grasp it at the time. Jesus often teaches us lessons that He knows we won't fully assimilate until later.

Try to grasp that Judas was not inhabited by any old demon from hell. Satan is not omnipresent. He can only be one place at a time. And for that time, he was in Judas. The prince of the power of the air flew like a fiery dart into the willing vessel of one of the Twelve. This proves that we can follow—closely—and still not belong to Jesus. We can talk the talk. We can blend right in. We can seem so sincere.

I believe through the videotape of his own retrospect, John saw the devil in Judas's eyes. I think he saw Satan in Judas's hands as he reached for the dipped bread. Think about it. For the briefest moment, two hands held the same bread. One soiled by silver; the other only a thin glove of flesh cloaking the hand of God. John saw the devil in Judas's feet as he walked away . . . for if we are ever truly with Christ, we cannot leave Christ.

Two-thirds of a century later, John would write, "They went out from us, but they did not belong to us; for if they had belonged to us, they would have remained with us. However, they went out so that it might be made clear that none of them belongs to us" (1 John 2:19). We learn some of our best, and worst, life lessons at the table. John learned this lesson at the table. He learned all too well.

Praying God's Word Today

Father, Your Word has warned us that men from among ourselves will rise up with deviant doctrines to lure Your disciples into following them (Acts 20:30). But Lord, our desire is that we would no longer be little children, tossed by the waves and blown around by every wind of teaching, by human cunning with cleverness in the techniques of deceit. Rather, speaking the truth in love, let us grow in every way into Christ, who is the head (Eph. 4:14–15). Sanctify us by the truth; Your word is truth (John 17:17).

DAY 17

Strength Personified

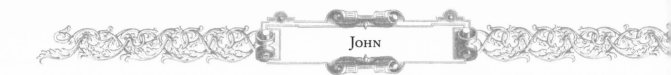

BEFORE YOU BEGIN

Read Matthew 26:36–46

STOP AND CONSIDER

Taking along Peter and the two sons of Zebedee,
He began to be sorrowful and deeply distressed. (v. 37)

Have you ever seen someone you consider to be a rock in unabashed anguish, virtually inconsolable, overwhelmed with sorrow? What impact did it have on you? _____

_____

_____

Can genuine strength and deep emotion dwell in the same person? How does seeing this in Jesus challenge your view of what steadiness and resiliency are made of? _____

_____

_____

_____

I have studied this scene many times before but never from the point of view of the disciples. Imagine that you are one of the three. Consider what Jesus had represented to them for the past three years. He certainly represented security and strength. Grown men don't follow for three years with virtually no income unless they are completely taken with the leader. I believe Jesus was their whole lives. In Him their pasts made sense. Their present was totally immersed in Him, and all their hopes for the future rested in His faithfulness to do what He promised. And indeed He would . . . but never in a million years would they have expected how.

"My soul is swallowed up in sorrow—to the point of death. Remain here and stay awake with Me" (Matt. 26:38).

Wait a second! This was their Rock! Their Strong Tower! "What in the world is wrong with Him? Why is He on the ground like that? Why is He writhing in anguish? Why is His hair drenched in sweat? It's freezing out here! And why does His sweat look like blood drops falling to the ground? Why does He keep asking for a cup to be taken from Him? What cup? He's crying 'Abba!' What's He so upset about? Is it because one of us betrayed Him? Why won't He stop? I hate seeing someone cry like that. I thought nothing could get to Him. Why won't He stop?"

The disciples may not have realized that Jesus was no less God that moment than He was on the Mount of Transfiguration or when He raised the dead. Their Rock and their Strong Tower was not falling apart. He was falling on His knees. That takes strength. Christ knew what He was going to have to do when He came to earth. He is the Lamb slain from the foundation of the world. He was as good as dead from the beginning. Jesus lived for one purpose alone: to do the will of His Father. Yet He still felt.

We are not wrong to feel. We are only wrong to disobey. Ask for the cup to be removed, but resolve to do His will. That's why He drew the three close enough to see. To teach them to pray . . . not sleep . . . in their anguish. This time they slept. But a time would come when each would rise from his own Gethsemane and bear his cross.

Praying God's Word Today

Lord, Your people have long known the feeling of sorrow—like Jeremiah, who cried out in lament for Your suffering people: "My anguish, my anguish! I writhe in agony! Oh, the pain in my heart! I cannot be silent" (Jer. 4:19). I know life is serious, Lord. My enemies are vigorous and powerful. I am attacked for pursuing good. But I also know that You will never abandon me, my God. Do not be far from me. Hurry to help me, Lord, my Savior (Ps. 38:19–22), for my hope is in You. When I cry, I cry out to You. _____

_____

_____

_____

_____

_____

_____

_____

_____

_____

_____

DAY 18

Mother and Son

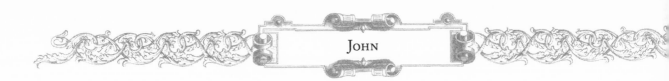
BEFORE YOU BEGIN
Read John 19:17–27

STOP AND CONSIDER

When Jesus saw His mother and the disciple He loved standing there,
He said to His mother, "Woman, here is your son." (v. 26)

How do you imagine the fulfillment of this responsibility played itself out over the course of John and Mary's remaining years? _____

_____

_____

What responsibilities has the Lord placed upon you? And just as this one was between John and Mary, how are your responsibilities expressions of His care for you and others?

_____

_____

_____

Have you ever looked around you at circumstances you could never have imagined experiencing and thought, "How did we get here?"—days that you desperately wish you could drop off the calendar so you can just go back to life as it was?

I believe that such experiences give us some concept of the way John must have felt in the scene depicted in the nineteenth chapter of his Gospel.

Can you imagine how John's head must have been spinning? Don't you know he wished someone would wake him up from his nightmare? Then came a profoundly tender and emotional interchange between Jesus, John, and Mary. Jesus assigned John to care for Mary, but be sure that you don't tag it as a warm and fuzzy moment and try to snuggle up to it. The events John observed were horrific. We can only appreciate the depth of the tenderness against the backdrop of the horror.

After beating Jesus within inches of His life, they held His hands and feet against the crude wood and fastened Him there with a hammer and three long nails. Whether or not John saw the pounding of the hammer, heaven could hear the pounding of his heart. At a time when any thinking man would want to run for his life, the youngest of all the disciples stayed.

Near the cross. That's what the Gospel of John says. Above the young man hung his world. His hero. His attachment. His future. His leader. Love of his life. Three years earlier he had been minding his own business trying to gain his daddy's approval with a boat and a net. He hadn't asked for Jesus. Jesus had asked for him. And here he stood. Isaiah's startling prophecy tells us that by the time the foes of Jesus had finished with Him, His appearance was disfigured beyond that of any man, and His form marred beyond human likeness (Isa. 52:14).

"When Jesus therefore saw his mother and the disciple standing by, whom he loved, he saith unto his mother, Woman, behold thy son!" (John 19:26 KJV). Don't take it lightly. Hear it. Not the way the passion plays do it. Hear the real thing. Hear a voice erupting from labored outburst as Jesus tried to lift Himself up and draw breath to speak.

Every word He said from the cross is critical by virtue of the fact that Jesus' condition made speaking harder than dying. Chronic pain is jealous like few other things. It doesn't like to share. If a man is in pain, he can hardly think of anything else, and yet Jesus did—perhaps because the pain of His heart, if at all possible, exceeded the pain of His shredded frame. The look of His mother's face. Her horror. Her suffering.

Jesus gazed straight upon the young face of the one who was standing nearby. John's face. Less than twenty-four hours earlier, this face had nestled against His chest in innocent affection. John, like our Melissa, was the baby of the family . . . and he knew it. He no doubt reveled in its privilege. If anyone had an excuse to run from the cross, perhaps it was John, and yet he didn't.

> At a time when any thinking man would want to run for his life, the youngest of all the disciples stayed.

Jesus saw the disciple whom He loved standing nearby. I believe indescribable love and compassion hemorrhaged from His heart. "Then saith he to the disciple, Behold thy mother! And from that hour that disciple took her unto his own home" (John 19:27 KJV).

If the cross is about anything, it is about reconciliation. "For he himself is our peace, who has made the two one and has destroyed the barrier, the dividing wall of hostility" (Eph. 2:14 NIV). The unbelief of Christ's brothers had raised a wall of hostility between them and His disciples. As Christ gazed upon His beloved mother and His beloved disciple, He saw His own two worlds desperately in need of reconciliation and a woman who no doubt was torn between the two. Simeon's prophecy to Mary was fulfilled before Jesus' very eyes: "A sword will pierce your own soul" (Luke 2:35). How like Jesus to start stitching a heart back together even as the knife was tearing it apart. One day soon His family and His disciples would be united, but the firstfruit of that harvest stood beneath the cross of Christ. "From that hour the disciple took her into his home."

How perfectly appropriate! Right at the foot of the cross we discover the very quality that set the apostle John apart from all the rest.

I am reminded of an Old Testament saint about whom God said, "My servant Caleb has a different spirit and follows me wholeheartedly" (Num. 14:24 NIV). God didn't mean a different Holy Spirit. All of us who are redeemed have the same Holy Spirit. No, God was referring to something wonderful about Caleb's own human spirit that made him unique. I believe John had something similar. These were fallible men prone to the dictates of their own flesh just like the rest of us, but they had something in them that was almost incomparable when overtaken by the Holy Spirit. They were simply different.

This question is hard for most of us to answer, but think of it as a tribute to God and His gifting grace rather than self-promotion. What has He made "simply different" about you? And how can you use this to bring honor to Him? _____

_____

_____

_____

_____

_____

_____

PRAYING GOD'S WORD TODAY

I know, Lord, that You are able to make every grace overflow to me, so that in every way, always having everything I need, I may excel in every good work You have placed before me (2 Cor. 9:8). I stand today secure in both Your calling and Your equipping, trusting in Your Word, thankful that I can be complete in You (2 Tim. 3:17).

DAY 19

I've Been There

BEFORE YOU BEGIN

Read John 19:28–37

STOP AND CONSIDER

He who saw this has testified so that you also may believe.

His testimony is true, and he knows he is telling the truth. (v. 35)

What can you testify about Jesus, just from being near Him the last few days and weeks? Don't answer quickly and generally. Be thoughtful. Be specific. _____

_____

_____

What do you do when you can't explain what Jesus is doing—like when He hasn't stopped a tragedy, or when He's not lifting another's suffering? _____

_____

_____

_____

You and I have arrived at a red-letter moment on which much of the remainder of our journey hinges. I am convinced we've stumbled on the thing that set John apart and made him the fertile soil into which God could sow the seeds of such a Gospel, such epistles, and such a revelation.

John remained nearby Jesus whether his leader was on the Mount of Transfiguration or in the deep of Gethsemane's suffering. John leaned affectionately upon Him during the Passover feast but also followed Him into the courts for the trials. John clung to Jesus when He raised the dead, and he clung to Jesus when He became the dead.

John was found nearby when human reasoning implied his faithful Leader's mission had failed. He could not have comprehended that the plan of the ages was going perfectly. Yet he remained. He who looked upon a face that had shone like the sun (Matt. 17:2) was willing to look upon a face bloody and spit upon. He stayed nearby during both Christ's brightest and darkest hours. The young disciple knew Jesus in the extremities. John was willing to look when others would have covered their eyes, and he beheld Him. How can we behold what we are unwilling to see?

We cannot claim to know anyone intimately whom we've not known in the intensity of both agony and elation. Anyone with eyes willing to truly behold Jesus will at times be confused and shocked by what he sees. You see, if we're willing to be taken to the extremes of His glory where intimate knowledge is gained, we will undoubtedly see things of Him we cannot explain and that sometimes disturb.

Then comes the question: Will we walk away from Jesus when from human understanding He looks weak and defeated? Do you know what I mean by that question?

When based on earthly evidence, human reasoning is left to one of two harrowing conclusions: He is either mean or weak. Think, beloved, about what I'm saying. Will we cling when our human reasoning implies evil has defeated Him? Or that evil seems to be found in Him? Will we stand by faith when human logic says to run? That's what will make us different.

PRAYING GOD'S WORD TODAY

Thank You, Lord, for sending us Your Counselor—the Spirit of truth who proceeds from the Father. He testifies of You. And as a result, I too can testify to what I have seen and heard, because You have allowed me to be near You and to learn of You (John 15:26–27). Keep me close, Lord, and never stop teaching me more and more, that I may declare Your power and goodness as long as I live.

DAY 20

Improving Grounds

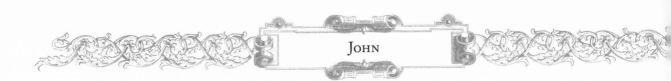
BEFORE YOU BEGIN

Read John 19:38–42

STOP AND CONSIDER

There was a garden in the place where He was crucified.

A new tomb was in the garden; no one had yet been placed in it. (v. 41)

How fitting that a garden was nearby the scene of such tragedy and loss. Besides the resurrection of Christ, what else have you seen grow up among the weeds of grief and despair?

_____

_____

What kind of cooperation is required from us if we are ever to experience tender shoots coming forth from the barren ground?_____

_____

_____

_____

Sometimes violent circumstances shake the earth beneath our feet. We feel as if a canyon has suddenly appeared and we've been hurled into it. Our emotions swing wildly, and we think we'll be torn in two. Those like Mary and John who loved Jesus most must have felt such a dichotomy of emotions at the finality of His death.

Watching someone suffer violent pain causes most loved ones to feel relief when it ends, even if death bid it cease. Then true to our self-destructive, self-condemning natures, relief often gives way to guilt. To add to the heap, the finality of the death ushers in feelings of hopelessness. Why? Because humanity has bone-deep indoctrination in the following statement: Where there is life, there is hope.

Not in God's strange economy. That day of all days, where there was death, there was hope. And strangely, even now for those of us in Christ, our greatest hope is in what lies beyond our deaths. We stand on the edge of our cliff-like emotions looking into the deep cavern of our grief, and we're sure that the jump will kill us. Yet for those of us who entrust our feeble selves to our faithful Creator, in ways I can neither explain nor describe, it doesn't. When death of some kind comes and we are willing to take it to the cross, to remain nearby, and to suffer its grief, we will also experience the resurrection.

We say, "But part of me has died with it." And indeed it has. Hear the words of Christ echo from the grave: "I assure you: Unless a grain of wheat falls into the ground and dies, it remains by itself. But if it dies, it produces a large crop" (John 12:24). As a child bearing the name of Christ, if a part of you has died, in time it was meant to produce many seeds. Oh, Beloved, don't give up!

We hear so much talk about the phases of grief: the shock, the anger, often depression, then, finally, acceptance. We're led to believe that acceptance of death is the final stage of grief. But if we are in Christ, the final stage has not come until we've allowed God to bring forth resurrection life and many seeds from the kernel of wheat that fell to the ground. Yes, we have to come to acceptance, but not just acceptance of the death. Acceptance of the resurrection life. Don't stop until you experience it. Though it tarry, it shall come!

PRAYING GOD'S WORD TODAY

Lord Jesus, You died and came to life for this: that You might rule over both the dead and the living (Rom. 14:9). And because we know that what we sow does not come to life unless it dies (1 Cor. 15:37), I give you every part of me today, knowing that even if death occurs, You have newness awaiting me.

DAY 21

Do-Bees

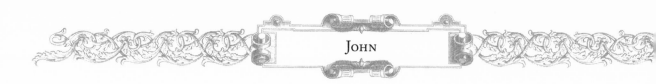

BEFORE YOU BEGIN
Read John 21:1–7a

STOP AND CONSIDER

"I'm going fishing," Simon Peter said to them. "We're coming with you," they told him. They went out and got into the boat, but that night they caught nothing. (v. 3)

What do you typically do when time is hanging heavy, spiritually speaking—when you're in that antsy, uncomfortable gap between asking for guidance and receiving direction?

_____

_____

The disciples found themselves in this same kind of "what do we do now?" spiritual limbo. What do you make of their decision to go fishing? _____

_____

_____

_____

Peter, Thomas, Nathanael, James, John, and two other disciples were all gathered in a fishing boat. My husband would tell you that seven men in your average boat is at least five too many, but Peter and the others had obviously returned to the commercial vessel where Peter had earned his living for years. He seems to have ascribed to this philosophy: when you don't know what to do, do what you used to do.

Even though the disciples must have been ecstatic to have Christ in their midst, I believe He purposely let those days become an identity challenge for them. Notice Jesus didn't hang around with them every minute He was back. He had appeared to the disciples only twice before this encounter (John 21:14).

The fact that Jesus didn't bind Himself to them during His brief post-resurrection tenure must have been confusing to them. I'm not sure they knew how they fit into Christ's plans from this side of the grave. Surely the thought occurred to them, "What need does anyone powerful enough to walk out of a tomb have for the likes of us?" They didn't understand that Christ's primary purpose during those forty days was for people to understand that He was God. Therefore, Jesus had more on His agenda than appearing only to the apostles. First Corinthians 15:5–7 lets us know Jesus appeared to over five hundred disciples.

But Psalm 46:10 tells us what to do when we're not sure where we fit in God's action plan. The psalm says, "Cease striving and know that I am God" (NASB).

Yep. Be still and know it ourselves. Don't default into our past. Don't jump the gun for our future. Just behold and know. Instructions will come when the time is right. In the meantime, just *be*—even though *being* is so much harder than *doing*, isn't it?

Thankfully, Jesus knew where to find His disciples anyway, and He interrupted their doing with His own being. John seemed to have a better grasp of what Christ had come to be than any of the others at this point. He is only attributed four words in this scene: "It is the Lord." Oh, that you and I would come to recognize what is the Lord and what is not.

PRAYING GOD'S WORD TODAY

Lord, the reason You have shown us such vivid proof of Your power is so we will know that You are God, that there is no other besides You (Deut. 4:35). Today I recognize and keep in mind that You are God in heaven above and on earth below. There is no other. So I will keep Your statutes and be faithful to Your commands (Deut. 4:39–40), resting in the knowledge of Your powerful reality until You show me the next path to take. _____

DAY 22

Diving in
the Deep End

Before You Begin

Read John 21:7b–14

Stop and Consider

When Simon Peter heard that it was the Lord, he tied his outer garment
around him (for he was stripped) and plunged into the sea. (v. 7b)

Can this kind of impetuousity ever square with mature Christianity? Under what conditions and situations do you find it called for? _____

_____

_____

What happens to those who lose (or never discover) their ability to cut loose with Jesus
every now and then? _____

_____

_____

_____

The second that John announced the stranger along the shoreline was indeed Jesus, Peter jumped from the boat and swam to Him with all his might. I realize our primary attentions are on John in this book, but I can't let this moment pass without putting the flashlight on one of Peter's sterling moments.

In our Christian circles we so often surround ourselves with people of similar practice of faith. We have our unspoken codes. Spiritual practices that we consider acceptable. We also agree on things that are not. Things that are weird. Behaviors that are just, well, overboard. Then someone jumps ship and decides he or she doesn't care what the rest of us think. Nothing is going to get between him and Jesus.

Glory! As much as I love John, in this scene I want to be Peter!

Actually, I remember well when I began to break the unspoken code of just how far my church compadres and I would go with this "spiritual thing." Years ago, those closest to me charged me with going overboard far more disapprovingly than others. Do you know what, though, Beloved? I wouldn't climb back in that boat for anything. How about you? Have you jumped out of the boat of what is most comfortable and acceptable and decided you want Jesus even if you have to make a fool of yourself to get to Him? If not, are you ready? What's holding you back?

Let me warn you. Intimacy with Christ doesn't always feel warm and fuzzy. Just ask Peter. That water was cold! This scene would have taken place during the latter part of our month of May. The days are very warm in that part of Galilee, but the temperature drops dramatically during the night. Mind you, this fishing trip took place before breakfast (John 21:12). No wonder the rest of the disciples followed in the boat!

I believe Jesus esteemed Peter's impetuous determination to get to his Lord. I am also convinced that this act was an important part of Peter's restoration. Notice he didn't ask to walk on water. He was willing to dog paddle in ice water to get to Jesus this time.

Praying God's Word Today

Lord, You reached down from on high and took hold of me. You pulled me out of deep waters (Ps. 18:16). For this if nothing else, I dive headfirst today into the deep waters of worship. Yes, my enemy was too strong for me, confronting me in the day of my distress, but You were my support. You brought me out to a wide-open place and rescued me because You delighted in me (Ps. 18:17–19). What incredible, unthinkable grace! Receive today my unrestrained praise.

DAY 23

Love Goes Around

BEFORE YOU BEGIN

Read John 21:15–23

STOP AND CONSIDER

When Peter saw him, he said to Jesus, "Lord—what about him?"

"If I want him to remain until I come," Jesus answered, "what is that to you?" (vv. 21–22)

The commentaries aren't sure, so we can speculate. Do you think Peter's question was out of deep concern for John, or did it arise out of jealousy or some other negative emotion?

_____

_____

Can you think of a time when you've asked a similar question? What was your motivation for doing so? _____

_____

_____

_____

Ambition could not supply the motivation to follow Jesus where Peter would have to go. In John 21, Jesus repeated the one motivation that would suffice. Jesus said to him three times, "Simon, son of John, do you love Me?" (John 21:17).

Oh, beloved, can you see the significance? No other motivation will last! We might feed the sheep or serve the flock based on other motivations for a while, but only one thing will compel us to follow the Lord Jesus Christ faithfully to the death: *love!*

You see, our callings may differ, but if we're going to follow Jesus Christ in the power of the crucified life, our compellings will be the same. Only love compels to the death. Circumstances will inevitably happen in all our lives that will defy all discipline, determination, and conviction. Opposition will happen. Life will get hard. Only love will keep burning when everything else disintegrates into an ashen heap. Pray for this one thing more than you pray for your next breath. I am convinced love is everything.

But I wasn't the first one convinced. I simply follow in a long line of believers who failed their way into the discovery that love is the highest priority and motivating force in the entire life of faith. Generations before any of us wised up, a young disciple named John was so drawn to Christ's discourse on love that he couldn't help but listen as Jesus and Peter walked away from the others to talk.

I am convinced the conversation recorded in John 21:15–23 began in the group of eight. Perhaps in the course of the question and answer, however, Jesus quite naturally stood up, brushed Himself off, and took a few steps away from the small circle of men. Peter, unnerved by his own interpretation of the repetitive question, probably jumped to his feet and followed.

Verse 17 tells us that Peter was "grieved" because Jesus questioned his love a third time: "Lord, you know everything! You know that I love you." Mind you, he was still drenched to the bone from his zeal. Jesus then prophesied the reason why Peter's love for Him would be so critical. Peter would be asked to glorify God by giving his own life. Only love would make him willing. Then, as if to say, "Knowing all this and with your eyes wide open," Christ reissued the call, "Follow me!" Don't downplay it for an instant. The cost of the call was huge.

We don't know what caused Peter to suddenly look behind him and see John following them. Perhaps John stepped on a branch that had fallen to the ground. Perhaps he groaned audibly when he heard Christ foretell his closest friend's future. But I don't believe John trailed them out of selfish curiosity. I think he sensed the enormity of the concept the risen Teacher was teaching through this emotional interchange.

Opposition will happen. Life will get hard. Only love will keep burning when everything else disintegrates into an ashen heap.

This was no tiptoed eavesdropping. I think he was drawn to the conversation like a magnet. I believe Scripture will prove that John, perhaps like no other disciple in that circle, assimilated the profound implications of what his beloved Savior was saying. "You are My called ones. You have tough futures ahead of you, but the glory God will gain will be immeasurable. Love is the only motivation that can afford this kind of cost."

When Peter saw John, he asked, "'Lord—what about him?'" Oh, at times like these, how I wish we had the Bible in its completely inspired and original form on videotape! We would be far better equipped to interpret a scene accurately if we could see the expressions on the face of the speaker and hear his tone of voice. Since we have no such help, words like Peter's may have as many different interpretations as I have commentaries. I'm looking at two different commentaries right this moment, and each says something different about Peter's motivation for asking this question.

No matter what your interpretation may be, I think we all can admit that the question plagues each of us at times, whatever our reason for asking. Perhaps God has called you to suffer some pretty difficult circumstances while another seems to flourish in relative ease. Or perhaps your heart has broken for someone who works so hard and serves so dili-

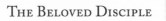

gently, but difficulty is her constant companion. Maybe one of your children has seemed so blessed and gifted by God and you keep looking at the other and asking, "Lord, what about him?"

Beloved, over and over Jesus tells us, "You can trust Me!" In this scene He is saying to His present-day disciples, "You can trust Me with you, and you can trust Me with them. I am the same God to all of you, but I have a different plan for each of you. You won't miss it if you keep following. Remember, I've been a carpenter by trade. Custom blueprints are My specialty. God's glory is My goal. Now fill your canteen to the brim with love and follow Me."

Victory often awaits our acceptance of the fact that God operates with His children on a need-to-know basis. If one of your current struggles involves comparing your plight with another's prosperity, how could love change the equation and lead you on to freedom?

Praying God's Word Today

I know that nothing good lives in me—that is, in my flesh (Rom. 7:18). So if I am to love others in genuine, kingdom-minded ways, it can only be Your love, Lord Jesus, that compels me. And when molded by and modeling Your love, I can come to this conclusion: One died for all—so that we should no longer live for ourselves but for You, who died for us and was raised (2 Cor. 5:14–15). This is the kind of heart You can enable me to have.

DAY 24

Going and Coming

Before You Begin

Read Acts 1:1–11

Stop and Consider

Why do you stand looking up into heaven? This Jesus, who has been taken from you into heaven, will come in the same way that you have seen Him going into heaven. (v. 11)

If you had seen Him taken into heaven—as John did—would a day ever pass that you didn't glance up and wonder when He was returning? How real is that expectation to you?

_____

_____

What should our attitude be toward the sure return of Christ? How does the operation of daily life coincide with the reality that He could appear before the day's out? _____

_____

_____

_____

Luke begins the Book of Acts, the companion volume to the Gospel of Luke, at the end of Christ's earthly tenure. Luke tells us Jesus had showed Himself to be alive "by many convincing proofs, appearing to them during 40 days and speaking about the kingdom of God" (Acts 1:3). Now at the end of that time, Christ and His disciples gathered at the Mount of Olives.

Try to imagine being one of the eleven on the hillside that day. Verse 11 seems to imply they were all standing, so imagine that they were basically eye to eye with Jesus, not letting a single word from His mouth fall to the ground. Jesus promised them the power of the Holy Spirit. Then without warning the disciples realized that they were glancing somewhat upward as He seemed a tad taller. As He rose a head above them, surely some of them looked down and saw that His feet were no longer on the ground. Luke 24:50 tells us Christ was blessing them as He lifted off the ground. Can you imagine what they were thinking and feeling?

Perhaps by now your imagination has drawn a rough sketch of the apostle John on the canvas of your mind. Picture him and the others bug-eyed with their mouths gaping open. Had my grandmother been one of the disciples (a frighteningly funny thought), she would have stood there saying, "Now, don't that just beat all?" I feel sure they said something comparable in Aramaic.

Just about the time they might have tried to rub the supernatural sight out of their eyes, God threw a cloudy cloak of *shekinah* glory over His beloved Son and swept Him home. Oh, don't you know the Father had been watching the clock of earth for that precious moment to finally arrive? While Christ was no prodigal, He was most assuredly a son who had journeyed to a foreign land. I can almost hear the Father say to His servants, "Quick! Bring out the best robe and put it on him; put a ring on his finger and sandals on his feet. Then bring the fattened calf and slaughter it, and let's celebrate with a feast, because this son of mine was dead and is alive again" (Luke 15:22–24). Had the angels not broken the stare, the remains of eleven stiff carcasses might still be on the Mount of Olives today.

Praying God's Word Today

Hallelujah, Lord Jesus! Come the day when You Yourself will descend from heaven with a shout, with the archangel's voice and the trumpet of God, and the dead in Christ shall rise. Then those who are still alive—be it we or a future generation—will be caught up together with them in the clouds to meet You, Lord, in the air. And so we will always be with You, at home in Your visible presence. Oh, how encouraged I am by this thought and these words! (1 Thess. 4:16–18). Come quickly—oh, come quickly, Lord Jesus!

DAY 25

Spiritual Connections

Before You Begin

Read Acts 1:12–14, 2:1–8

Stop and Consider

When the day of Pentecost had arrived, they were all together in one place.
Suddenly a sound like that of a violent rushing wind came from heaven (vv. 1–2).

We can look back and see these events fulfilling prophecy and making history. But we, too, are in the midst of God's sovereign will and timing. Are you seeing any evidence of that?

_____

_____

Yes, we walk by faith, but our faith rests on the rock-solid, historical facts of Crucifixion, Resurrection, Ascension, and Pentecost. How do these set Christianity apart? _____

_____

_____

_____

You are probably very familiar with the scene described in these verses, but sometimes overfamiliarity can be the biggest treasure thief of all. Rewind the verses again, and let's play them in slow motion.

Scripture tells us the disciples' return to the city after observing Christ's ascension on the Mount of Olives was a "Sabbath day's journey" (Acts 1:12), which would have been about three-fourths of a mile. I have walked that brief trek a number of times, and it is straight downhill until you ascend back up the temple mount to the city gates. You can hardly keep from walking fast due to the incline, but somehow I'm imagining their mouths were traveling faster than their feet. (You're imagining that mine was too!)

We read that the disciples went upstairs to the room where they were staying (Acts 1:13). The definite article and the emphatic arrangement of the words in the Greek sentence structure indicate that the location was well-known and highly significant to the disciples.[5] In the days that followed, the now eleven apostles were joined for prayer by several women, Mary, and Jesus' siblings. Acts 1:15 shows Peter speaking to that first New Testament cell group that numbered 120 people.

You may attend a church about this size and wonder with frustration what God could do with such a small group of people. Dear One, when the Holy Spirit falls on a place, it doesn't matter how small the group—things start happening! Remember, the Holy Spirit comes in order to get results! And in light of Acts 2, we know what can happen when the Holy Spirit interrupts a prayer meeting.

Now I want you to come with me on one of my favorite journeys. Open your Bible to Leviticus 23—(I'll wait on you)—and look at the headings that appear there, if your Bible contains those. This awesome Old Testament chapter records the annual feasts God appointed to Israel. I am convinced every one of them is ultimately fulfilled in Jesus Christ. In the context of this chapter, we'll emphasize three.

The most important of the Jewish feasts was (and is) Passover (Lev. 23:4–8). I so love the last few words in 1 Corinthians 5:7—"Christ our Passover has been sacrificed."

We can easily see the connection that Jesus is the fulfillment of all the Passover lambs slain in history. What a glorious connection between the Old and New Testaments!

The feast that immediately followed Passover was Firstfruits, when a sheaf of the first grain of the harvest was waved before the Lord for His acceptance (Lev. 23:11). This was the day after the Passover Sabbath, obviously falling on a Sunday. First Corinthians 15:20 clearly says that the resurrection of Jesus was the firstfruits. "Now Christ has been raised from the dead, the firstfruits of those who have fallen asleep."

Fifty *(pente)* days after Passover came the Feast of Weeks, later called Pentecost. It was the celebration of seven weeks of harvest. The one sheaf waved on Firstfruits turned into an entire harvest celebrated seven weeks and one day later. "But each in his own order: Christ, the firstfruits; afterward, at His coming, the people of Christ" (1 Cor. 15:23). The Feast of Weeks was the presentation of an offering of new grain to the Lord (Lev. 23:16). In other words, it was the celebration of harvest reaped.

> We are left here for the distinct purpose of becoming witnesses to an injured world in desperate need of a Savior.

Now do you see the significance of what happened on Pentecost? Fifty days earlier, Christ the Passover Lamb had been crucified. On the day of Firstfruits—that very Sunday morning—His life was waved acceptable before God as the firstfruit from the dead. Fifty days after Pentecost, the Holy Spirit came just as Christ promised. And He came to show off! He revealed His all-surpassing power in simple jars of clay that day. The Holy Spirit never comes just to show off, however. He comes to show off and bring results: "Every day the Lord added to them those who were being saved" (Acts 2:47).

Beloved, I present to you the first harvest reaped by the life, death, and resurrection of Jesus Christ our Lord. That's Pentecost! And even now I believe we are still living in the continuing harvest of Pentecost. Christ tarries only so that the harvest can reach its peak ripeness and be reaped to the glory of God. He does not will for any to perish but for all to come to repentance (2 Pet. 3:9). He desires everyone. He forces no one. He will not wait forever.

One day the ultimate Feast of Trumpets (Lev. 23:23–24; 1 Thess. 4:16) will come, and we will meet Jesus in the air. Then one day the books will be opened and closed for the last time, and the final judgment will take place (Rev. 20:11–15). The Day of Atonement will be past (Lev. 23:26–27; Rom. 3:23–25). Those who were covered by the blood of the Passover Lamb will tabernacle (Lev. 23:33–34) with God forever and ever . . . and so shall we ever be with the Lord (1 Thess. 4:17).

I feel like getting started a little early. I'm going to go put on some praise music, and I may just slip on my dancing shoes!

Are you not amazed to see spiritual history in such perfect, prophetic alignment? With God's wisdom so immense and His plan so secure, how will you respond the next time you're tempted to think that His Spirit is less powerful in you today than He was then?

_____

_____

_____

_____

_____

PRAYING GOD'S WORD TODAY

Lord Jesus, Your voice has gone out to all the earth, and Your words to the ends of the inhabited world (Rom. 10:18). The weight and gravity of Your truth are simply too massive to ignore. Therefore, I choose to remain grounded and steadfast in the faith, not shifted away even one inch from the hope of the gospel (Col. 1:23). It is God's power for salvation to everyone who believes (Rom. 1:16). It is the story of my redeemed life. _____

DAY 26

Beggars in
Beautiful Places

BEFORE YOU BEGIN

Read Acts 3:1–10

STOP AND CONSIDER

When he saw Peter and John about to enter the temple complex, he asked for help.
Peter, along with John, looked at him intently and said, "Look at us." (vv. 3–4)

The beggar "saw" Peter and John, but the inference is clear he didn't really look at them.
Why is it hard for beggars—like we all are sometimes—to look into the face of help?

_____

_____

What keeps you insulated from the dire reality of human need? What are you afraid of
seeing or being asked by God to do? _____

_____

_____

_____

What you have in this chapter of Scripture is a pair of mighty fine servants. Allow me to highlight a few things I love about Peter and John in this scene.

1. *They cherished their heritage.* Please don't miss the fact that the New Testament church was Jewish! According to Acts 2:46 the believers met daily in the temple courts. Acts 3 opens with Peter and John on their way to the three o'clock prayer time at the temple, which coincided with the evening sacrifice. The thought never occurred to them to cast off their Judaism for their new faith in Christ. For heaven's sake, Jesus was Jewish! Nothing could have been more absurd. Their Messiah had fulfilled their Jewish heritage. They were no longer obligated to the letter of the Law because Christ had met its righteous requirements. They were free, however, to enjoy its precepts and practices as expressions of their faith in Jesus.

Can you imagine how belief in Christ and their newfound knowledge of Jesus as the answer to every symbolic practice spiced up their participation? Suddenly the black-and-white of their ritual prayer services turned Technicolor with the life of the Spirit. I snicker when I think of observers at Pentecost thinking the disciples must have been drinking. Don't you know they secretly wanted a sip of whatever the believers were having?

Try to grasp this, though: God cherishes your heritage, too. You may balk, "What are you talking about? My past is horrible!" Listen carefully, Beloved. We are no longer under the law and authority of our pasts, but like Peter and John we are also free to use them as they lend expression to our faith in Jesus. As much as you might not want to hear this, you couldn't become the servant God is calling you to be without the threads of your past being knitted into the Technicolor fabric of your future.

Still not convinced? Perhaps you're thinking, "I'd take Peter and John's Jewish heritage over mine any day!" Wonderful! Because in addition to your own, you have their heritage, too! Behold what Galatians 3:29 says about you: "If you are Christ's, then you are Abraham's seed, heirs according to the promise." I love that Peter and John cherished their heritage.

2. *Peter and John understood true religion.* They were not so busy getting to prayer meeting that they missed the beggar at the gate. Don't miss the significance of the location at the gate called Beautiful. Leave it to God to appoint a bitter reality in our "beautiful" scene. Try as we may to avoid the misery, misfortune, and injustice around us, they will find us, even in cities filled with gated, extravagant "planned communities" with walls around them to keep the niceties in and the unpleasantries out.

> We are no longer under the law and authority of our pasts, but like Peter and John, we are free to use them as they lend expression to our faith in Jesus.

Peter and John could have glanced at the nearest sundial and said, "Oops! We're almost late for prayer meeting. Beg on, brother!" Instead, Peter looked straight at the man as did John (Acts 3:4). Refreshing, isn't it? I'm not much for looking suffering and poverty straight in the face. I'll face it, all right. But I like to look slightly to one side or the other. Not Peter and John. They looked straight at him and likewise demanded that he look straight at them.

3. *Peter and John gave what they had.* I love the words in the King James: "Silver and gold have I none; but such as I have give I thee: In the name of Jesus Christ of Nazareth rise up and walk" (Acts 3:6). God never asks us to give what we don't have! Somehow I'm relieved by that assurance.

4. *Peter took him by the hand and helped him up.* Peter and John knew better than anyone that the power to heal the man came solely from the Holy Spirit. The man wasn't healed because Peter took him by the hand and helped him up. To me, the tender representation here is that Peter offered the man a handful of faith to help him get to his feet. After all, this man had been crippled all his life. What reason did he have to believe he could be healed? All he thought he wanted was a little money. When the beggar grabbed on to Peter's hand, he felt the strength in his grip. The confidence of his faith. In one clasp, Peter offered a handful of faith, and that was all the man needed to come to his feet.

Oh, Beloved, can you see him? Close your eyes and watch! Watch the beggar jump to his feet, his tin cup tumbling down the temple steps and the few measly coins spinning in the afternoon sunshine. Look at the expression on his face! Watch him dance on legs thin from atrophy. Look! Look straight at him! That's him jumping and praising God through the temple courts. Laugh over the horrified expressions on pious faces. Look for the others in the crowd who are ecstatic with joy and decide to grab a handful of faith for themselves.

5. *Peter and John took no credit for the miracle.* After all, if man can do it, it really isn't a miracle, now is it? Miracles are from God . . . for the likes of crippled man. Someone reading today has been begging God for trivial things like silver and gold when God wants to raise her to her feet to jump, dance, and praise Him. Why do we want God to help us stay like we are? Grab a handful of faith and be changed!

Which of these observations struck the strongest chord in your heart? Write what God is showing you about it. _____

_____

_____

_____

_____

_____

_____

PRAYING GOD'S WORD TODAY

I praise You today, Lord, that although You were rich, for our sakes You became poor, so that by Your poverty we might become rich (2 Cor. 8:9). And now may we, though poor in ourselves, be able to enrich many through the grace You have given us. For although we have nothing, in You we possess everything (2 Cor. 6:10).

DAY 27

Muzzles into Megaphones

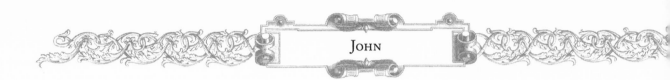
BEFORE YOU BEGIN
Read Acts 8:1–13

STOP AND CONSIDER
So those who were scattered went on their way
proclaiming the message of good news. (v. 4)

When have you had an experience that seemed like a setback, yet God sovereignly used it to accomplish spiritual progress in your heart and put a fresh word of testimony in your mouth? _____

_____

_____

In fact, when has ease and comfort ever drawn you closer to Jesus? Describe your walk with God when things are going smoothly. _____

_____

_____

_____

Earlier in the book of Acts, we witnessed the New Testament church gathering often for prayer in the temple courts. But the disciples soon faced a virtual end to their freedom to practice their faith unafraid on temple grounds, as the religious leaders threatened Peter and John "not to preach or teach at all in the name of Jesus" (Acts 4:18).

Over the next several chapters, persecution increased like stones pummeled from the fists of a crazed mob. The reality of the religious establishment's intentions rose frighteningly to the surface as Stephen fell to his knees. I am convinced he was bloodied and bruised by a gnawing and growing paranoia in their souls: What if they were wrong about Jesus of Nazareth? What if they did crucify the Son of glory? They would do everything they could to silence the mouths of those who made them question their own actions.

But the Sanhedrin underestimated the tenacity of Christ's unschooled and ordinary followers, who in effect inverted their muzzles and made them megaphones. Acts 8:1–4 tells of God's unusual method of spreading the gospel. In *The Two St. Johns of the New Testament*, James Stalker wrote, "Not infrequently it was by persecution that the new faith was driven out of one place into another, where, but for this reason, it might never have been heard of; so that the opposition which threatened to extinguish the fire of the Gospel only scattered its embers far and wide; and wherever they fell a new fire was kindled."[6]

What amazing providence! When Christ told His disciples that they would receive power and become witnesses not only in Jerusalem but to the uttermost parts of the earth, they never expected His means! No, His ways are not our ways. Our ways would always be comfortable. Convenient. Certainly without hurt or harm. We would always ask that God use the favor of man to increase our harvests. Not the fervor of opposition.

If you've walked with God very long, I have little doubt He has used what you perceived as a very negative means to achieve a positive result. I suspect that God has allowed you to experience a fence pushed down painfully in your life to expand His horizon for you. God is faithful, isn't He? Even when He turns the ignition on a holy bulldozer to plow down a confining fence.

PRAYING GOD'S WORD TODAY

Like Paul—whom you used, oddly enough, to be a leading cause of scattering the early believers—I want to be able to say that I am grateful for difficult times, knowing that they actually result in the advancement of the gospel (Phil. 1:12) and a fresh sense of dependence upon You. Therefore, I will not be ashamed when trouble comes, hoping that now as always, with all boldness, You will be highly honored in my body, whether by life or by death (Phil. 1:20).

DAY 28

Do I Know You?

BEFORE YOU BEGIN
Read Acts 8:14–25

STOP AND CONSIDER

When the apostles who were at Jerusalem heard that Samaria
had welcomed God's message, they sent Peter and John to them. (v. 14)

Why is it so much easier to dislike people from a distance? What do we usually fill in for
what we don't know about others? _____

_____

_____

What do you really know about a person or group of people whom you may stereotype or
judge? How willing are you to take a chance that God could change your mind? _____

_____

_____

_____

Does the location of Samaria and its relationship to John ring a bell of any kind to you? The first bell this reference probably rings is the word Christ spoke over the eleven disciples in Acts 1:8 before His ascension. I'd like to suggest that when Christ made the proposal that His disciples would be witnesses in Samaria, He raised a few eyebrows. Jerusalem? No problem. Judea? Absolutely. Ends of the earth? We're Your men, Jesus. But Samaria? Jews despised the Samaritans! If Gentiles were the target of the Jews' prejudices, then the Samaritans were the bull's-eye. And the feelings were mutual. Samaritans were considered by most Jews to be a mongrel breed. They were border people who lived in the strip of land between the Jews and the Gentiles. The Jews didn't associate with the Samaritans (John 4:9).

The idealists among us might be thinking, "But surely since they followed Christ, the disciples didn't have those kinds of prejudices toward people." Luke 9:51–56 gives a far more realistic picture. Our friends James and John wanted to call down fire on a Samaritan village because of a small slight. Don't assume they were being overdramatic and didn't really mean what they were saying. That Jesus took great offense to their suggestion is clear as He turned on His heels and gave them a swift rebuke.

Yes, Jesus saw something lethal in James and John's hearts that day. But instead of threatening His childish followers with a dose of their own medicine, Jesus chose a far more effective route. In Acts 8:14, Jesus arranged to assign John to be an ambassador of life to the very people he volunteered to destroy. Don't think for an instant John's assignment was coincidental. Even as the words fell from Jesus' lips in Acts 1:8, He may very likely have looked straight at John when He said, ". . . and Samaria."

Earlier I mentioned our naïveté to think followers of Christ are automatically void of prejudices. Whether our preferred prejudices are toward denominations, people of other world religions, colors, or economics, they are usually so deeply ingrained in us that we just see them as "the way we are" rather than as sin. But make no mistake—prejudice is sin. The prejudgment and stereotype of a grouping of people is sin. Plain and simple.

One of God's redemptive tools for dealing with prejudice is appointing His guilty child to get to know a person from the group she or he has judged. I was reared in one denomination and had very few if any relationships in my young life with anyone outside of it. Much prejudice evolves from pure ignorance, and I grew up judging some groups of people that I simply didn't understand. But God wasn't about to let me stay in my bubble, because He intended to develop in me a heart for the entire body of Christ. His redemptive way of accomplishing His goal was to place me in the position of getting to know others who practiced their Christian faith in ways that differed from mine.

> One of God's tools for dealing with prejudice is appointing His guilty child to get to know a person from the group she or he has judged.

The most obvious work God did in my life involved a woman from one of those churches that my old church would have considered maniacal and unsound. I was in my twenties and "accidentally" developed a friendship with her before I knew where she went to church. I fell in love with her heart for God. She had such a love for His Word, and we boasted in Him often and developed a deep friendship.

When I found out her denomination, I was stunned. She wasn't crazy. She wasn't a maniac. She wasn't unsound. When my other friends would make fun of people from that church, I couldn't bring myself to join in anymore. The jokes weren't funny.

I don't think for a second John missed the point when the apostles sent him and Peter to the Samaritans. He came face-to-face with them. They, too, were created in the image of God. They, too, loved their children and worried over their welfare. They, too, bruised when they were hit and wept when they were sad. They seemed so different from a distance. Somehow, up close and personal, they didn't seem nearly so . . . weird. Then

something really amazing happened. "Peter and John laid their hands on them, and they received the Holy Spirit" (Acts 8:17).

Well, well, well. They got their wish after all. They *did* call down fire on the Samaritans. The kind of fire that destroys things like hate. Meanness. Prejudice. For those who let this Holy Fire consume them. The kind of fire that destroys the old and births the new. Our God is a consuming fire, and that day He lit the hearts of Samaritans at the hands of Jews.

I want to say something that sounds simple, but it is so profound to me right at this moment: How I praise God that we—sinful, selfish, ignorant mortals—can change. John wasn't stuck with his old prejudices. God neither gave up on Him nor overlooked the transgression. God was gracious enough to push the envelope until change happened. Acts 8:25 concludes the segment by saying that Peter and John "traveled back to Jerusalem, evangelizing many villages of the Samaritans." How like Jesus. He turned John's prejudice into a fiery passion.

What is one way that God has dramatically changed your attitude toward a target of your own personal prejudice? If you don't have an answer to this, I'd encourage you to seriously consider your heart. _____

_____

_____

_____

_____

PRAYING GOD'S WORD TODAY

Father, You have convicted me deeply today about loving my enemies—even those whom I myself have made my enemies. For if I love those who love me, what credit is that to me? Even sinners love those who love them and are like them (Luke 6:32). Actually, we all were once foreigners to the covenants of promise, with no hope and without God in the world. But now in Christ Jesus, we who were far away have been brought near by the blood of Christ. For You are our peace, who made both groups one and tore down the dividing wall of hostility (Eph. 2:12–14). May I be an instrument for tearing down the walls.

DAY 29

No! No! No!

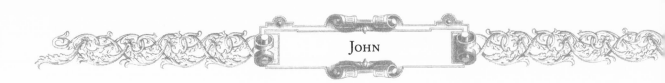
BEFORE YOU BEGIN
Read Acts 12:1–5

STOP AND CONSIDER

About that time King Herod cruelly attacked some who belonged to the church,
and he killed James, John's brother, with the sword. (vv. 1–2)

Inseparable as boys, death had now separated James and John. Try to articulate his feelings and reaction. Perhaps, sadly, you know it from personal experience. _____

_____

_____

Think of it, too, in terms of the young mission they were on for Christ. How could this possibly square with what He had called them to do? _____

_____

_____

_____

I have studied and even taught Acts 12 many times. I love the story of Peter's deliverance from prison, but I had never before regarded the events from John's point of view. How devastated he must have been!

By this time in the Book of Acts, the disciples all knew the Jews could make good on their threats. They had crucified Christ and stoned Stephen. They told Peter and John to stop speaking in the name of Jesus or else.

They chose "or else." Acts 8:1 tells us that a persecution had scattered the believers, but the apostles remained in Jerusalem. Yes, John and Peter trekked to Samaria, but the ministries of the apostles remained intact in Jerusalem for this period of time. I assume that they simply did not yet feel released by the Holy Spirit to center their ministries elsewhere.

Now in a terrible wave of persecution, James was arrested. I wonder if John saw them seize his brother. If not, who broke the news to him? Can you imagine the sear of terror that tore through his heart? Remember, John was the apostle who'd had connections when Jesus was arrested and was able to get into the priest's courtyard. Don't you know he tried to pull every favor and call on every connection he had? He probably couldn't sleep. He couldn't eat. He no doubt fell facedown on the floor and begged God to spare his brother's life.

Beloved, don't hurry past this scene. James was John's flesh and blood. All the disciples were terrified, but none of them could relate to John's horror. Surely prayer meetings took place. Don't forget, these were men with the power and authority of the Holy Spirit to heal diseases and cast out demons. No doubt they named and claimed James's release and demanded his life in prayer. For all we know, James claimed his *own* life before his jailers and forbade them to harm one of Jesus' elect. After all, the disciples were promised power and were told they would be Christ's witnesses all over Jerusalem, Judea, Samaria, and the uttermost parts of the earth. His ministry had just begun! No, this couldn't be the end. He would surely be delivered!

Then they killed him.

I pity the person who came to John with the news. In 2 Samuel 1, David was so horrified by the report of Saul and Jonathan's deaths that he had the bearer of bad news slain. Although John had no such authority or desire, don't you imagine he wanted to shake the bad news out of the bearer's mouth and demand a different ending? Don't you also imagine that he tried his hardest to shake the reality out of his own head? James was the first of the disciples martyred. Reality must have hit like an unsuspected tidal wave, crashing on the shores of servant lives.

> Sometimes we don't realize how real God is until we've experienced the awesomeness of His answerless Presence.

More than any of the other ten, John must have replayed the events a thousand times in his mind, wondering if his big brother had been terrified or calm. Did he think of their parents? Hadn't Zebedee been through enough? How was he going to tell his mother? Had James felt any pain? Was it quick? Was he next? Then before he had time to steady from reeling, he learned he was not next. Peter was.

Have you ever felt like a percussionist had just slammed king-size cymbals on both sides of your head? "Not Peter! This was too much! Not James *and* Peter! Not both of them, Lord! Please, please, no, Lord!"

Perhaps John's mind flew back to that time on the lake shore when "Peter turned around and saw the disciple Jesus loved following them. . . . When Peter saw him, he said to Jesus, 'Lord—what about him?'" (John 21:20–21)

"Yeah, Lord! What about me? How will I go on through all of this without James and Peter? What are You doing? What *aren't* You doing? Will You let them kill all of us?"

John had good reason to believe Peter might never make it out of that prison. But then he did. God granted him a miracle . . . scarcely before they had mopped the blood of John's big brother off the floor. Can you imagine the mix of emotions John must have felt if he was anything like the rest of us?

When you grapple with questions like, "Why did God let the blood of my brother spill but performed a miracle for my best friend?" the explanations of others only frustrate you more. In fact, often we only bother asking so we can release a little anger in the demand of a better answer. Rarely will it come.

Solitude is not so much the place we find answers. It's the place we find our own square foot of earth from which to grapple with heaven and decide if we're going on—possibly alone—without our answers. And many of us will. Why? Because the privilege of wrestling with such a holy and mysterious God still beats the numbness—the pitiful mediocrity—of an otherwise life. Sometimes we don't realize how real He is until we've experienced the awesomeness of His answerless Presence. He knows that what we crave far more than explanations is the unshakable conviction that He is utterly, supremely God.

Will you loosen your hold on anything and anyone else as prerequisites of following Him? Are you willing to be faithful, even when it means being faithful alone? How dependent are you on others for your allegiance to Christ? _____

_____

_____

_____

_____

_____

PRAYING GOD'S WORD TODAY

Lord God, in those times when I fight to reconcile the facts of life with the words of faith, I depend on the fact that You give strength to the weary and strengthen the powerless. Youths may faint and grow weary, and young men stumble and fall, but those of us who trust in You will renew our strength. We will soar on wings like eagles. We will run and not grow weary. We will walk and not faint (Isa. 40:29–31)—not just when things are going well but when everything inside me feels like giving up and shutting down.

Day 30

How Do I Know
I Can Trust You?

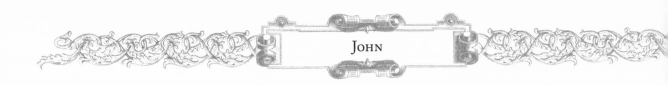
BEFORE YOU BEGIN
Read Acts 9:19b–31

STOP AND CONSIDER
When he arrived in Jerusalem, he tried to associate with the disciples,
but they were all afraid of him, since they did not believe he was a disciple. (v. 26)

What would John have probably thought about someone who threatened to murder Christians one minute, then become one of them the next? _____

_____

_____

What has been your experience with people who promise dramatic changes in their lives? How do trust and caution coexist in equations like these? _____

_____

_____

_____

You may wonder what the persecutor-turned-preacher named Saul had to do with our protagonist. Actually, Paul's testimony will offer us several important insights into the apostle John and also will supply us with a very valuable time line.

In Galatians, Paul tells that after his conversion he went to Arabia and then returned to Damascus. Only after three years did he travel to Jerusalem. The three years encompassed his original stay in Damascus, his flight to the desert, his return to Damascus, and his travel time to Jerusalem. Position John among the disciples in Jerusalem at this time.

But don't miss the words in Acts 9:1, where Saul was "still breathing threats and murder against the disciples of the Lord." Peter, John, and the others had plenty of reasons to take Saul's actions personally. Furthermore, they hadn't received the same vision God had given to Ananias in Damascus concerning the validity of Saul's conversion. Saul could have faked his conversion as a means of getting close to them and exposing their unrelenting evangelism after the warning to cease.

Fast-forward your thoughts on the time line now to the events surrounding the death of James, John's beloved brother. We have no reason to believe much time passed between Paul's conversion and the martyrdom of James. We know that Stephen was martyred before Paul's conversion and that Paul in fact gave approval to his death. James was martyred after Paul's conversion. Even though several years had passed, don't you imagine that if John were anything like most of us, he had some pretty strong feelings about Paul?

Even though Paul dramatically gave his life to Christ before James was seized and killed, had I been John, I would have had a fairly difficult time embracing him. I'm afraid I might have had thoughts like, "If not for people exactly like you, my brother might still be alive." Maybe John felt none of what I'm describing, but I believe Christ's first ragtag band of followers were like us. Yes, the Holy Spirit had come to them and, yes, they had matured somewhat, but grief and loss don't always perpetuate extremely rational feelings. None of the rest of the apostles had lost a blood brother at this point. I just have to wonder how John felt about Paul those first several years.

Praying God's Word Today

Father, I don't always see eye-to-eye with everyone who claims You as Lord. But You have set before us the goal of living our lives in a manner worthy of the gospel of Christ—standing firm in one spirit, with one mind, working side by side for the faith (Phil. 1:27). May I set my personal preferences aside and pour my heart into matters of greater importance, of kingdom importance.

DAY 31

The Right Hand
of Fellowship

BEFORE YOU BEGIN

Read Galatians 2:1–10

STOP AND CONSIDER

When James, Cephas, and John, recognized as pillars, acknowledged the grace that had been given to me, they gave the right hand of fellowship to me and Barnabas. (v. 9)

How well is the "right hand of fellowship" being extended in your church, especially with people of different viewpoints? What are some of the reasons why it is often withheld?

_____

_____

In what different ways can God give grace to a person? How, specifically, has He given His grace to you—not just in salvation but in other aspects of life? _____

_____

_____

_____

Picture the five men mentioned in Galatians 2:9 conferring together and giving approval to one another: James, the unbelieving mocker turned preacher; Peter, the one sifted like wheat, denying Christ three times, then having enough faith to return and strengthen his brothers; John, the Son of Thunder, who asked if he could sit at Christ's side in the kingdom and destroy the Samaritans with fire from heaven; Paul, a former religious madman who approved the murder of Stephen and helped fuel a persecution that resulted in James's death; Barnabas, the son of encouragement, who risked getting hammered by the early church by building a bridge between unlikely brothers.

That's just it. We're all unlikely brothers. In Christ's church, the pillars were never designed to match. Each one is distinct. What need would cookie-cutter disciples meet? None of us were meant to match. We were meant to fit together. Two identical puzzle pieces don't "fit." Oh, that we would celebrate that difference.

Do you remember what Paul said James, Peter, and John recognized in him that caused them to extend the right hand of fellowship? They "acknowledged the grace that had been given to me" (Gal. 2:9). First Peter 4:10 echoes the same concept: "Based on the gift they have received, everyone should use it to serve others, as good managers of the varied grace of God." Beloved, we don't have to agree on every single point of doctrine. We don't even have to always get along. We just need to recognize that grace has been given to us all.

To fulfill our kingdom purposes on earth, we could all use a right hand of fellowship from others, couldn't we? When I think back on those that God so graciously appointed to extend such a hand to me, I am deeply humbled and awed. I have been asked countless times how John Bisagno, the longtime pastor of my home church, handled this ministry coming out of his church. Beloved, he didn't just handle it. He pushed it! For years the only reason people invited me to come to their church was because they trusted him!

Did Brother John know I had a lot to learn? Perhaps more than anyone else. So did my mentor, Marge Caldwell. Did he agree with everything I taught or did? I doubt it. Yet they both continued to work with me, give me a chance to grow, and let me develop into my own person and not cookie-cutter images of them. They each extended me the right hand of fellowship for one reason. They recognized the grace of God in my once broken life.

When LifeWay approached me with a contract to tape the first series, *A Woman's Heart: God's Dwelling Place*, I was pitifully wet behind the ears. I don't know much about what I'm doing now, but I assure you I knew nothing then. I was petrified. The enemy came against me with such conflict and fear, I think I would have backed out had I not signed a contract. I felt like I needed advice desperately and needed someone to tell me whether my feelings were normal.

> What need would cookie-cutter disciples meet? We were not meant to match. We were meant to fit. Two identical puzzle pieces don't "fit."

I still feel like an idiot over what I did next, but I was desperate. I called Kay Arthur's office and asked to speak to her. I had no idea what I was doing. I had never seen her in person or had the privilege of taking one of her courses. Don't get the idea that I in any way saw a comparison. I just wanted to talk to a woman who had taught the Word on videotape no matter what gulf of knowledge and experience separated us.

But God wasn't about to let me get in touch with Kay Arthur. First of all, He wanted me to rely on Him alone. Furthermore, He knew He had already extended the right hand of fellowship to me through sufficient people. I also believe God knew how extremely impressionable I was at that time and that I had not yet allowed Him to fully develop my style. I have so much respect for Kay that if I could have, I would have wanted God to make me just like her. What need whatsoever would God have had for such a thing? Kay does an excellent job of being Kay, so why on earth would God have wanted me to approach Bible study in exactly the same way? He already had her!

Today I could pick up the phone and call Kay, and we could laugh and talk for an hour if we had the time. But through the years both of us felt the call of God to do something far more public. Each of us has gone out of our way to demonstrate that we are united in

Christ Jesus and we serve the same God . . . albeit with different styles. I have taught some of her books. Kay has invited me to several of her conferences to lead prayer and to speak. She has extended to me something more precious than gold: the right hand of fellowship. She knows I have a lot to learn. We wouldn't agree on every interpretation. She is simply a woman who recognizes grace when she sees it. I am so grateful.

Fourteen years lapsed between the time Paul first tried to fit in with the apostles and when he finally received the right hand of fellowship. I'd like to suggest the hand didn't come a moment behind schedule. What use would God have had for Paul if he simply turned out to be another James? Another Peter? Another John? His mission was distinct. And so, Beloved, is yours. God knows what He's doing! Trust Him. God is busy making you someone no one else has ever been.

What is the risk involved in letting God call and equip His people just the way He desires? But what is the hazard of trying to make other believers act and think only the way *we* want them to? _____

_____

_____

_____

_____

_____

_____

Praying God's Word Today

You are teaching me that there are different gifts, but the same Spirit; different ministries, but the same Lord; different activities, but the same God who is active in everyone who loves You and everything invested in Your kingdom (1 Cor. 12:4–6). You have placed the parts—each one of them—in the body just as You wanted. If they were all the same part, where would the body be? (1 Cor. 12:18–19). So in love and humble submission, may I extend grace and fellowship to others, just as You have extended the same to me.

DAY 32

Under the Radar

BEFORE YOU BEGIN
Read 1 John 2:24–27

STOP AND CONSIDER
If what you have heard from the beginning remains in you,
then you will remain in the Son and in the Father. (v. 24)

What do routine and boredom tend to do to your enthusiasm for serving Christ? How dependent are you upon noticeable results and recognition? _____

_____

_____

What are some of the spiritual and relational jewels that can be unearthed during seasons of sameness? _____

_____

_____

_____

Acts 12:2 is the last mention Luke makes of John as he refers to his brother's death. I am very intrigued by the fact that Luke mentions John only a handful of times in the annals of the early church—and never quoted him. Our dear protagonist appears only as an aside to Peter. While the book of Acts traces almost every move of a converted persecutor named Saul, John's ministry continues with very little notice after James's death.

I wonder what the apostles thought about Paul gaining so much of the spotlight. I think we'd be pretty naïve to think they didn't notice. John may also have felt that Peter at least had an important future, even if it ultimately required his life. John, on the other hand, knew nothing about his own. All he may have known was that Peter's ministry was skyrocketing, and no one would argue that Paul was a household name.

John? Christ simply asked him to take care of his mother. Goodness knows he loved her. He took her into his home just like he promised, but somehow in the midst of the responsibility, neither Scripture nor traditions give us any indication he ever had a family of his own. Of course, to have known Mary so well was to gain priceless insight into Christ. After all, who knew Him better? Surely she recounted stories as the evening oil in the lamp grew scarce. Scripture paints John as curious, so I can't imagine that he failed to ask a thousand questions through the years. "What did Gabriel look like when he brought the news? Did you know instantly he was an angel? What was his voice like?" Or, "Did you almost lose hope that James and your other sons would ever believe?" If Mary was like most aging mothers, I imagine she told the stories all the more and perhaps even repetitively as her life hastened toward its end.

Many of the early church historians agree that John resided in Jerusalem until Mary died. I wonder what Mary's home-going was like. If John and Christ's half-brothers had any notion she was dying, they were no doubt by her side. A natural death must have been so different to the eyewitnesses of the resurrected Lord Jesus. They knew firsthand the reality of life beyond the grave. Can you imagine how anxious Mary was to see her first-born son?

I have little doubt that those nearby reassured her through her final hours with words of their imminent encounter. Like all of us, God counted her steps and kept her tears in a bottle. Both were full and it was time. As He narrowed that solitary life to an earthbound close, He could easily see beyond the weathered face lined by time.

I like to think Mary was surrounded by loved ones as she inhaled her last ounce of earthly air. I imagine her sons gathered around her. All of them. The one she adopted at the cross and the One she surrendered to the grave. I wonder if they knew their Brother was right there among them . . . more present in His invisibility than they could ever be. Mary bid farewell to mortality and was ushered to immortality on the arm of a handsome Prince. Her Son. Her God.

> Peter's ministry was skyrocketing, and Paul was a household name. John? Christ simply asked him to take care of his mother.

John's job was done. What now? Perhaps he did what we sometimes do. When I am confounded by what I don't know, I rehearse in my mind what I do know. He knew that the last thing Christ told the apostles was that they would be witnesses in Jerusalem, Judea, Samaria, and the uttermost parts of the earth. I am of course offering supposition, but I wonder if he thought to himself, "I've served here in Jerusalem for years. I've preached to Samaritans, and I know Judea like the back of my hand. I'm no longer a young man. Who knows how much longer I have? I'm heading to the uttermost."

Beloved, listen. Christ's early followers were adventurers! They were pioneers! If they listened to us sit around and decide whether we had time to work in a Bible study with prison inmates around our nail appointments, they'd be mortified. In our postmodern era, church life is associated with buildings and programs. Church life to them was moving in the adrenaline and excitement of the Holy Ghost at the risk of life and limb. They were willing to do things we would reason couldn't possibly be the will of God (i.e., risking our necks) for the sheer joy of what lay before them. They ran the race. They didn't window shop.

I'm not meaning to be harsh, but I fear they might look at all of us and think virtually none of us looked like disciple material to them. But you know what I'd want to say to that first motley crew? "None of you looked like disciple material either when Christ dragged you from your safe little lives." My point? We can still become disciple material! I desperately want to! I want to live the Great Adventure. Don't you? Even if that Great Adventure leads me into virtual obscurity for a while.

We are built for adventure. And often, the only thing keeping us from embarking on one is that it's come disguised as an average day. What kind of adventure with Christ might be awaiting you before sundown tomorrow if you were looking for it? Just imagine . . .

PRAYING GOD'S WORD TODAY

Lord Jesus, You have surrounded us with a large crowd of witnesses—like Paul, like Peter, like John, like others in our own generation—who inspire us to lay aside every weight and the sin that so easily ensnares us, and to run with endurance the race that lies before us, keeping our eyes on You, the source and perfecter of our faith, who for the joy that lay before You, endured a cross and despised the shame, and have sat down at the right hand of God's throne. So I think of You today—one who endured such hostility from sinners against Yourself—so that I won't grow weary and lose heart (Heb. 12:1–3).

DAY 33

Insecure Identities

Before You Begin

Read 1 John 3:18–22

Stop and Consider

If our hearts condemn us, God is greater
than our hearts and knows all things. (v. 20)

When you're weak, down, or tired, what old temptations does Satan often try to reawaken in your fleshly nature? _____

_____

_____

If you only went on what your heart was telling you, what would you believe about your current circumstances? And what would your heart *not* tell you? _____

_____

_____

_____

Did John start doubting his identity and his significance somewhere along the way? Peter was no doubt the front-runner in Jerusalem and the early church. Next to him, the book of Acts implies James, the half-brother of Christ, was most prominent. Furthermore, John went to Ephesus and built on the foundation laid by none other than Paul, the former persecutor and latecomer onto the scene.

You may be thinking, "But what difference does that make?" In an ideal world, none. But this is no ideal world. In the dead of the night when insecurities crawl on us like fleas, all of us have terrifying bouts of insecurity and panics of insignificance. Our human natures fall pitifully to the temptation at times to pull out the tape measure and gauge ourselves against people who seem far more gifted and anointed by God.

John went on to outlive every other apostle while all of them were counted worthy to give their lives for the sake of Christ. Did he ever wonder if he were too unimportant to even be considered a threat enough to kill?

We may want to think he was surely too mature and filled with the Holy Spirit to have such thoughts, but keep in mind this is the same disciple who asked to sit at one of Jesus' sides in the kingdom. Yes, John was a new creature, but if Satan worked on him anything like he works on me, he targeted his weak times and hit him again with the same brand of temptations that worked in the old days. John's old fleshly desires for significance had been goliath. I can't imagine Satan not trying to pinpoint them again.

One way we have to respond is by choosing to believe what we know rather than what we feel. If John struggled with his identity in the era of the early church, that's exactly what he must have done. We know because of the virtually incomparable fruit produced after years of relative obscurity. In spite of others seeming more powerfully used by God and in the midst of decades hidden in the shadows, John remained tenacious in his task.

No doubt remains in my mind that God spent this time testing and proving John's character so he could be trusted with the greatest revelation. The answers God is willing to give us in our tomorrows often flow from our faithfulness when we have none today.

Praying God's Word Today

Lord Jesus, I know there is no such thing as obscurity to You. The eyes of El Roi ("the God Who Sees"—Gen. 16:13) gaze approvingly upon every effort and ounce of faith I exercise in Your name. Lord, You have encouraged us to continue in the faith—even in times of discouragement—by telling us, "It is necessary to pass through many troubles on our way into the kingdom of God" (Acts 14:22). But knowing that I am not forgotten, and knowing that what lies ahead will be worth it all, I press on. Teach me to do Your will, for You are my God. May Your gracious Spirit lead me on level ground (Ps. 143:10).

DAY 34

Call of the World

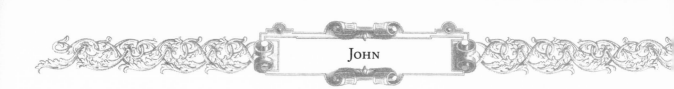
BEFORE YOU BEGIN

Read 1 John 2:15–17

STOP AND CONSIDER

Do not love the world or the things that belong to the world.

If anyone loves the world, love for the Father is not in him. (v. 15)

What are the most compelling "loves" in your life? Which of them come from the Father, and which from the world? _____

_____

_____

Some enjoyments only turn sinful when we let them get out of bounds. How do we keep this from happening—without becoming suspicious of anything that's fun or pleasurable?

_____

_____

_____

I stumbled upon a quote that I can't shake out of my head. "Saints . . . die to the world only to rise to a more intense life."[7] I've turned the quote over in my mind a hundred times, and I'm convinced it's true. John may be the perfect example. I believe God had something so divinely unique to entrust to this chosen apostle that He had to slay the call of the world in him. Mind you, not the call *to* the world but the call *of* the world.

I don't think John was so unlike Abraham or Moses. God chose these men but refined them for their tasks through the crucible of time and challenged trust. The obvious difference is that God used John mightily soon after his calling, but I'd like to suggest that his latter works fall into the category we'll call "greater works than these." As God sought to kill the world in His chosen vessels and crucify them to their own plans and agendas, their terms in waiting were not emptied and lifeless. Rather, their lives greatly intensified.

Our callings are not so different. We will never be of great use to God if we do not allow Him to crucify us to ourselves and the call of the world.

Our consolations, however, are exceedingly great! We trade the pitifully small and potentially disastrous for the wildest ride mortal creatures could ever know. We don't just die to self to accept nothingness. We lay down our lives and the call of the world to receive something far more intense. The call of God! The time spent awaiting further enlightenment and fuller harvest are meant to bulge with relationship.

Months then years then even decades may have blown off the calendar of John's life in biblical obscurity, but don't consider for an instant that they were spent in inactivity or emptiness. No possible way! Please do not miss the following point: During the interim years of biblical obscurity in John's life, one of the most intense relationships in the entire Word of God developed. Yes, Christ used John to cast out demons, heal the sick, and spread the good news through word of mouth. But somewhere along the way God built a man to whom He could entrust some of the most profound words ever recorded on parchment—all by a man once simply known as the "brother of James."

Praying God's Word Today

O Lord, may I not be conformed to the desires of my former ignorance, but rather, as You are holy—the One who has called me to Yourself in Christ Jesus—may I, too, be holy in all my conduct (1 Pet. 1:14–15). May I use the things of this world as if not engrossed by them, knowing that this world is passing away (1 Cor. 7:31 NIV), but that the word of our God remains forever (Isa. 40:8). _____

DAY 35

He Loves Me

BEFORE YOU BEGIN

Read 1 John 4:13–19

STOP AND CONSIDER

We have come to know and to believe the love that God has for us. God is love, and the one who remains in love remains in God, and God remains in him. (v. 16)

When you're feeling especially alone and unappreciated, how do you go about trying to grab an extra measure of love and acceptance? _____

_____

_____

What inevitably happens when you attempt to get all your needs met by someone else—your spouse, your friends, your children? Why do our needs exceed mortal fulfillment?

_____

_____

_____

Do you find it at all peculiar that John alone called himself "the one Jesus loved"? (John 13:23). If we believe the Gospel of John was inspired, however, then we must accept that the detail of John's self-identity was also inspired. Not because Jesus' love for John exceeded the others but because God purposed the reader to know how John saw himself. At first glance we might be tempted to think John a bit arrogant for terming himself such, but God would never allow a man who received such revelation to get away with that kind of self-promotion.

I'd like to suggest that John's evolving identity over the course of those decades came out of the opposite kind of heart. God is far too faithful not to have greatly humbled John before giving him such surpassing revelation. (See a parallel concept in 2 Cor. 12.)

I believe quite possibly the heightened positions of Peter and Paul in the era of the early church coupled with the impending martyrdom of each apostle fed abasement in John rather than exaltation. Surely he struggled with terribly perplexing feelings of fear that he, too, was doomed to martyrdom—and yet fear that he wasn't. Does that make sense?

But as the years went by and the virile, youthful fisherman grew old and gray, I am convinced that John's weakening legs were steadied and strengthened on the path by the constant reassurance, "Jesus, You chose me. You keep me. And above all else, You love me. You love me! No matter what happens or doesn't, Jesus, I am Your beloved."

If any of us had been John during the years conspicuously silent in Scripture, we might have given up. Or at least dropped into a lower gear. Not John. He knew two things, and I believe he grabbed on to them for dear life. He knew he was called to be a disciple. And he knew he was loved. Over the course of time, those two things emerged into one ultimate identity. "I, John, the seed of Zebedee, the son of Salome, the brother of James, the last surviving apostle am he: the one Jesus loves." Beloved disciple. Somewhere along the way, John, that Son of Thunder, forsook ambition for affection. And that, my friend, is why he was sitting pretty when some of the most profound words ever to fall from heaven to earth fell first like liquid grace into his quill.

PRAYING GOD'S WORD TODAY

You have told us, Lord, that Your beloved rests securely on You, that You shield him all day long and he rests on Your shoulders (Deut. 33:12)— that though the mountains move and the hills shake, Your love will not be removed from us, and Your covenant of peace will not be shaken (Isa. 54:10). Oh, satisfy us in the morning—every morning—with Your faithful love so that we may shout with joy and be glad all our days (Ps. 90:14).

DAY 36

I'm Full, Thank You

BEFORE YOU BEGIN
Read John 1:14–18

STOP AND CONSIDER
From the fullness of his grace we have all
received one blessing after another. (v. 16 NIV)

What do you just absolutely love about being in relationship with the living God? What
would be missing without Him? _____

_____

_____

The Bible tells us to "grow in the grace and knowledge" of Christ Jesus (2 Pet. 3:18). What
does growing in grace consist of? How does it change our attitudes and perspectives?

_____

_____

_____

John 1:16 introduces a key concept that will carry us through this vital part of our journey. I encourage you to memorize it! If you will receive what this verse is saying to you, your entire life experience with Jesus will be transformed.

The original word for "blessing" is *charis*, often translated "grace." This explains the King James rendering: "And of his fulness have all we received, and grace for grace." *Charis* is "that which causes joy, pleasure, gratification, favor, acceptance . . . a benefit . . . the absolutely free expression of the loving kindness of God to men finding its only motive in the bounty and benevolence of the Giver; unearned and unmerited favor."[8]

Based on John 1:14 and 1:16, then—and this definition—I believe we can accurately draw the following conclusions:

1. *Jesus is full of grace and truth.* He's the One and Only.

2. *All of us get to receive from His fullness!* Not just John the apostle. Not just John the Baptist. Jesus is full and overflowing with everything any of us who believes could possibly need or desire, and we get to receive from it!

3. *These grace gifts flowing from Christ's fullness* are not only beneficial, but they are expressions of God's favor that cause joy and pleasure!

It's high time I made a blatant confession. I am a Christian hedonist. Have been for years even before I knew what the term meant. I wish I had better words for it, but let me just say it like it is: Jesus makes me happy! He thrills me! He nearly takes my breath away with His beauty. As seriously as I know how to tell you, I am at times so overwhelmed by His love for me, my face blushes with intensity, and my heart races with holy anticipation. Jesus is the uncontested delight of my life.

I never intended for this to happen. I didn't even know it was possible. It all started with an in-depth study of His Word in my late twenties and then surged oddly enough with a near emotional and mental collapse in my early thirties. At the end of myself I came to the beginning of an intensity of relationship with an invisible Savior. No one had ever told me such a relationship existed. Now I spend my life telling anyone who will listen.

I thought I was just weird. I knew so many believers who wore Christ like a sacrifice that I thought I missed something somewhere. Don't get me wrong. Plenty of believers in the world make huge sacrifices in the name of Jesus Christ, but I'm not sure American believers can relate . . . and we can be a little nauseating when we try.

When we pursue Him feverishly and desire to love Him passionately, we will have an unexpected collision with joy and fulfillment.

By far the biggest sacrifices I've ever made were times I chose to pursue myself and my own will over Jesus and His. I'd be a liar to tell you Jesus has been some big sacrifice for me. He is the unspeakable joy and love of my life. In crude terms, I think He's a blast.

While still in the closet, I began stumbling on other Christian hedonists. Perhaps Augustine is the most blatant historical example. Of his conversion in 386, Augustine wrote, "How sweet all at once it was for me to be rid of those fruitless joys which I had once feared to lose! . . . You drove them from me, you who are the true, the sovereign joy. You drove them from me and took their place, you who are sweeter than all pleasure."[9] My heart leaps as I read words that I, too, have lived!

Jonathan Edwards was another. In 1755 he wrote, "God is glorified not only by His glory's being seen, but by its being rejoiced in. When those who see it delight in it, God is more glorified than if they only see it."[10]

C. S. Lewis was also a fine Christian hedonist. He wrote:

> If there lurks in most modern minds the notion that to desire our own good and earnestly to hope for the enjoyment of it is a bad thing, I submit that this notion has crept in from Kant and the Stoics and is no part

of the Christian faith. Indeed if we consider the unblushing promises of reward and the staggering nature of the rewards promised in the Gospels, it would seem that our Lord finds our desires not too strong, but too weak. We are half-hearted creatures, fooling about with drink and sex and ambition when infinite joy is offered us, like an ignorant child who wants to go on making mud pies in a slum because he cannot imagine what is meant by the offer of a holiday at the sea. We are far too easily pleased.[11]

Beloved, I don't care who you are or how long you've known Jesus, I am convinced we have hardly scratched the surface. So much more of Him exists! So much more He's willing to give us! Show us! Tell us! Oh, that we would spend our life in furious pursuit!

If, as John Piper says, "God is most glorified in us when we are most satisfied in Him,"[12] what would happen if you really started enjoying Him? What would be different if you thought of grace as God's favor looking for a place to happen? _____

_____

_____

_____

_____

_____

Praying God's Word Today

I pray, Lord, that You would grant me, according to the riches of Your glory, to be strengthened with power through Your Spirit in the inner man, and that Christ would dwell in my heart through faith. I pray that being rooted and firmly established in love, I might be able to comprehend with all the saints what is the breadth and width, height and depth, and to know the Messiah's love that surpasses knowledge, so that I may be filled with all the fullness of God (Eph. 3:16–19).

DAY 37

To Life!

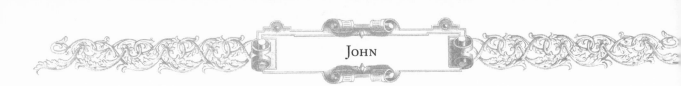
Before You Begin

Read John 1:1–5

Stop and Consider

Life was in Him, and that life was the light of men.

That light shines in the darkness, yet the darkness did not overcome it. (vv. 4–5)

Does the thought of having a great life make you nervous? How is it possible that such a thing could coincide with making His glory the sole purpose of your existence? _____

_____

_____

What types of "darkness" threaten to overcome the light that Jesus illumines within you?

_____

_____

_____

_____

Many inspired men in Scripture confessed the glorious gain of pursuing God, but few can compete with our very own apostle John. In the totality of John's writings and in a comparison of his Gospel with the three synoptics, John has more to say about the concepts of life, light, love, truth, glory, signs, and belief than anyone else in the entire New Testament.

John has overwhelmingly more to say about God as Father than any other inspired writer. In fact, out of 248 New Testament references to God as Father, John penned 130. In impressive balance, John also has more to say about God and the world than any other inspired writer. Of the New Testament references to the world, 103 out of 206 are John's. I could go on with many examples.

My point? It's certainly not that his Gospel is better than others. Each was inspired just as God perfectly intended. The point is that in length of life and depth of love, John discovered the concept of "more." In fact, I'm convinced that a nutshell explanation for John's entire experience and perspective is intimated in one of the most profound statements of Christ ever dictated to him. Jesus said, "I have come that they may have life and have it in abundance" (John 10:10).

Do you realize that Christ wants you to have a great life? Don't confuse great with no challenges, hardships, or even suffering. In fact, the greatest parts of my life experience have been overcoming the overwhelming in the power of the Holy Spirit. When we lay down these lives of ours, God wants us to be able to say we lived them fully. We didn't miss a thing He had for us. We had a blast with God. Just like John.

Jesus offered a lot of life; John took Him up on it. Jesus shed a lot of light; John chose to walk in it. Jesus revealed a lot of glory; John chose to behold it. Jesus delivered a lot of truth; John believed it. Jesus shed a lot of blood; John felt covered by it. Jesus lavished a lot of love; John received it. Jesus is full of everything we could ever need or desire. Thankfully, many receive, but others receive more abundantly. John was one of those.

PRAYING GOD'S WORD TODAY

Lord God, Your faithful love is so valuable, we can take refuge in the shadow of Your wings. Then we are filled from the abundance of Your house, and You let us drink from Your refreshing stream. For with You is life's fountain, Lord. In Your light we will see light (Ps. 36:7–9).

DAY 38

I Could Say More

BEFORE YOU BEGIN

Read John 21:24–25

STOP AND CONSIDER

There are also many other things that Jesus did, which, if they were written one by one, I suppose not even the world itself could contain the books that would be written. (v. 25)

If you had to boil down your testimony with Jesus to the few lines beneath this question, what would you say? How would you summarize it? _____

_____

_____

Do you have one Bible verse that you'd say is your favorite, the one you might call the theme of your life? If you don't already have it memorized, look it up and write it here.

_____

_____

_____

In the very early years of the New Testament church, Eusebius penned the following statement from Clement of Alexandria: "John, last of all, conscious that the outward facts had been set forth in the Gospels, was urged on by his disciples, and, divinely moved by the Spirit, composed a spiritual Gospel."[13] If Clement was accurate, John was familiar with the synoptic Gospels and had neither the desire nor a compelling of the Holy Spirit to repeat the biographical approach of Matthew, Mark, and Luke. The Gospel of John shares only about 10 percent of its content with the other Gospel writers. Clement did not mean all four were not equally inspired. He simply suggested that the last Gospel can draw us further into spiritual truths.

Though John's approach is vast and deep, my Greek teacher tells me that John's Greek is the most easily read of all the New Testament books. Perhaps Augustine had these facts in mind when he wrote, "John's Gospel is deep enough for an elephant to swim and shallow enough for a child not to drown."[14] So whether we're elephants or children in our relationship to the Word, you and I can splash to our delight in the living water of this Gospel.

Like several other New Testament books, the end of this Gospel explains why the book had a beginning. I never hear this verse (John 21:25) without thinking about my first guide in Israel who told me that the ancient Hebrews often spoke in pictures and images. He said, "For instance, we would read John's intent in this final verse like this: 'If all the trees of the forest were quills and the oceans ink, still they could not record all Jesus did.'" Ah, yes! That's my kind of wording!

Whatever your preference in rhetoric, we can conclude from John's ending that the elements shared in the pages of his Gospel were purposefully selected by the leadership of the Spirit working through the personality and priorities of John. No other Gospel writer surpasses his determination to express Jesus' absolute deity. John wrote his Gospel so that the reader would behold truth from an utterly convinced eyewitness that Jesus Christ is the uncontested Christ. The Messiah. The Son of God.

Praying God's Word Today

Lord, You have given me hope through Your Word. It is my comfort in every affliction—Your promise has given me life (Ps. 119:49–50). And though I am so often forgetful of all that You have done for me, and too quick to go negative in spite of Your boundless grace, Your statutes are the theme of my song during my earthly life (Ps. 119:54). Teach me new lyrics of Your love with each passing day, and may I sing it aloud in every circumstance.

DAY 39

Believe It

Before You Begin

Read John 20:24–31

Stop and Consider

These are written so that you may believe Jesus is the Messiah,
the Son of God, and by believing you may have life in His name. (v. 31)

"Believe" is a verb—an action word, a term that denotes forward movement and thinking.
What are you "believing" in Jesus the Messiah today? _____

_____

_____

See, belief is more than doctrinal points and position summaries. Why did John think this
was so important to get across—that "believing" was the only way to experience "life"?

_____

_____

_____

In his book *Encountering John*, Andreas J. Kostenberger wrote:

> Apart from "Jesus" and "Father" there is no theologically signifi-
> cant word that occurs more frequently in John's Gospel than the word
> "believe" (*pisteuo*; 98 times). . . . Another interesting observation is
> that while John uses the verb "to believe" almost a hundred times, he
> does not once use the corresponding noun (*pistis*, "faith"). It appears
> therefore that John's primary purpose is to engender in his readers the
> act of believing, of placing their trust in Jesus Christ.[15]

Glory to God! John's Gospel doesn't just call us to belief, as if it were in the past tense and complete. In Christ we are called to be living verbs, Beloved! We are called to the ongoing act of believing! Yes, for many of us the belief that secures our salvation is past tense and complete. In other words, we have already trusted Christ for salvation, and we are now and forever secured. But tragically too many live in past-tense belief, believing God for little more from that time forward.

Believing in Christ and believing Christ can be two very different things. We begin with the former, but we certainly don't want to end there! We want to keep believing what Jesus says about Himself, His Father, and us until we see Him face-to-face.

Think of the roll call of the faithful in Hebrews 11. As eternally vital as faith is, none of these were commended for the initial faith that enabled them to enter a relationship with God. Rather, they were commended for ongoing acts of believing at times when their physical eyes could not see what God told them they could believe.

It's by no coincidence either that the same Gospel that speaks so often about the act of believing also includes the word "life" more than any other. Any of those in the great cloud of witnesses of Hebrews 11 would tell us that really living the Christian life is synonymous with really believing the God who created it.

PRAYING GOD'S WORD TODAY

I am so grateful, Lord, that from the beginning You have chosen me for salvation through sanctification by the Spirit and through belief in the truth (2 Thess. 2:13). But I am equally awed and inspired to realize that You, the God of hope, are even now filling me with all joy and peace in believing, so that I may overflow with hope by the power of the Holy Spirit (Rom. 15:13). Oh help my unbelief—and help me to believe!

DAY 40

John's Jesus

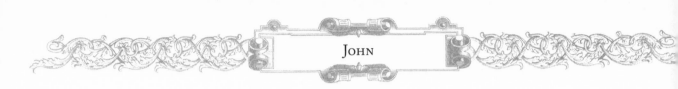

BEFORE YOU BEGIN

Read John 1:6–13

STOP AND CONSIDER

But to all who did receive Him, He gave them the right to be
children of God, to those who believe in His name. (v. 12)

From where or from whom have you received much of your understanding of who Jesus is?
What have you learned about Him from these people, experiences, and sources? _____

_____

_____

Throughout the pages to come, we'll study John's Jesus, full of grace and truth. If your life
were a Gospel like John's, who could people "believe" your Jesus to be? _____

_____

_____

_____

John's Jesus is the same One who is meant to be ours: the preexistent, miracle working, only begotten Son of the Father of all creation. Years ago God revealed to me that I believed in my childhood church's Christ, who (thankfully) was a Savior for sinners, but I had hardly begun to believe in the Bible's Christ. Yes, He is a Savior for sinners and so much more! We have derived a staggering amount of our impressions of Christ from vastly incomplete if not totally unreliable sources, as sweet and respectable as they may be!

We are blessed beyond measure for every time one of these human instruments extended us reliable impressions of Jesus. I derived most of my early impressions about Jesus based not so much on what I *learned* at church as what I *saw* at church. I certainly believed Jesus saves, and that belief led me to my own salvation experience. But I believed Him for little more because I saw evidence of little more. The few marvelous exceptions marked me forever, but I wonder why so many believers believe so little of Jesus. I'm just going to say it like I see it. Either Jesus no longer does what the Bible says He did, or we don't give Him the chance.

John went out of his way to present us an all-powerful Son of God who speaks and His Word is accomplished. A Savior who not only saves us from our sins but can deliver us from evil. A Great Physician who really can heal and a God of glory who reveals His magnificence to mere mortals. And, yes, a God of signs and wonders. We've already seen John testify that one of his chief purposes in his Gospel was to testify to the signs Jesus performed so that readers would believe—not in the miracles themselves, mind you, but in the Christ who performed them.

Many claim, "The day of miracles has ceased." I don't doubt that God may employ miracles less frequently in cultures where the Word of God is prevalent, but I know Jesus Christ still performs miracles. The first reason I know this to be true is from the claims of Hebrews: "Remember your leaders who have spoken God's word to you. As you carefully observe the outcome of their lives, imitate their faith. Jesus Christ is the same yesterday, today, and forever" (Heb. 13:7–8).

The second reason I know Jesus Christ still performs miracles is because I'm one of them. I'm not being dramatic. I'm telling you the truth. The only excuse for an ounce of victory in my life is the supernatural, delivering power of Jesus Christ. I was in the clutches of a real, live devil, living in a perpetual cycle of defeat. Only a miracle-working God could have set me free then dared to use me. Scripture suggests no greater work exists. According to the apostle Paul in Ephesians 3:20, God "is able to do above and beyond all that we ask or think—according to the power that works in you." Do you see, Beloved? The most profound miracles of God will always be those within the hearts and souls of people. Moving a mountain is nothing compared to changing a selfish, destructive human heart.

Sometimes we see little because we believe little. That's the obstacle you and I want to overcome so that we can live in the abundant blessing of Jesus Christ.

Third, I know Jesus Christ still performs miracles because I've witnessed them. I have seen Him do things most people I know don't even believe He does anymore. Jesus healed a woman I know personally from liver cancer and a man I know personally from pancreatic cancer. I've seen women bear healthy children who were diagnosed inside the womb with debilitating conditions. I was in a service with a dear friend in his eighties who has been legally blind for years when God suddenly restored a remarkable measure of his sight—right on the pew of a Baptist church! Hallelujah!

Like you, I have also seen many who have not received the miracles they hoped for. I can't explain the difference except to say that God often defers to the greater glory. Sometimes the far greater miracle is the victory He brings and the character He reveals when we don't get what we thought we wanted.

On the other hand, sometimes we see little because we believe little. That's the obstacle you and I want to overcome so that we can live in the abundant blessing of Jesus Christ.

When my life is over, I may not have seen Jesus perform some of the miracles the Word says He can—but let it be because He showed His glory another way and not because I believed Him for so pitifully little that I didn't give Him the chance!

When we received Christ as our Savior, you might picture that a pipe of power connected our lives to God's throne. Unbelief clogs the pipe, but the act of believing clears the way for the inconceivable! As much as John's Gospel has to say about believing, I'm not sure anyone recorded a more powerful statement than Mark. He tells us Jesus said, "Everything is possible to the one who believes" (Mark 9:23).

Through His work on the cross and His plan before the foundation of the world, Christ has already accomplished so much for your life in heaven! But if His work is going to be accomplished here on earth where your feet hit the hot pavement, you're going to have to start believing Him—the Jesus of the Scripture.

What holds you back from believing—from believing who He really is, how much He really loves, and what He can really do? _____

_____

_____

_____

_____

_____

Praying God's Word Today

I love You, Lord Jesus, even though I haven't seen You. And though not seeing You now, I believe in You, rejoicing with inexpressible and glorious joy because I am receiving from You the goal of my faith, the salvation of my soul (1 Pet. 1:8–9). I have put my hope in You, the living God, the Savior of those who believe (1 Tim. 4:10)—the same One who is so much more to those of us who continue to believe. Thank You, Lord, for being my . . .

DAY 41

Party On

BEFORE YOU BEGIN

Read John 2:1–5

STOP AND CONSIDER

On the third day a wedding took place in Cana of Galilee. Jesus' mother was there,
and Jesus and His disciples were invited to the wedding as well. (vv. 1–2)

John was most likely an adolescent when he witnessed Jesus enjoying this festive occasion.
What do you think a teenager would have made of this scene? _____

_____

_____

What reasons might Jesus have had for turning down this invitation? How could partying
be a wise use of His time, right here at the outset of His earthly ministry? _____

_____

_____

_____

I believe Jesus didn't have to have His arm twisted to attend a wedding. I happen to think He loved a good party. Still does. I am convinced Jesus' basic personality in His brief walk in human flesh was delightful and refreshingly relational.

You remember, for example, that Jesus made the disciples allow children to come to Him (Matt. 19:14). It's pretty obvious that children aren't drawn to cranky people. The Scripture also tells us that Jesus' critics complained about His eating with tax collectors and "sinners" (John 5:30) and about seeing Him partying rather than fasting (Matt. 9:14).

Why in the world have we let "partying" become associated with licentiousness? God created man and formed within him an authentic soul-need to feast and celebrate. In fact, God deemed celebration so vital, He commanded His people to celebrate at frequent intervals throughout the calendar year (Lev. 23). Let me say that again: He *commands* that we celebrate His goodness and His greatness!

So I say it's time we take the whole idea of partying back. I'm always mystified that many nonbelievers think Christians must be dull, bored, and wouldn't know a good time if it socked them in the noggin. Boy, do we have a secret! No one laughs like a bunch of Christians! My staff and I roll with laughter together at times.

I even remember a time when three of my dearest friends and I scrunched on one couch together, all holding hands. One of us had lost a daughter several days earlier to a drunk driver. But as we held on to one another for dear life, God gave us the sudden gift of the hardest belly laugh any of us had enjoyed in a long time. Unbelievers might be insulted to know that when we go to their parties, we wonder why they think they're having such a good time. (Lean over here closely so I can whisper: *I think they're boring.*)

The primary reason why celebrations around Christ's presence are so wonderful is because they are the kind intended to be sparkling refreshment to a world-worn soul. We get to attend Christ's kind of parties without taking home a lot of baggage. We don't have a hangover later or a guilty conscience. Christ-centered celebrations are all the fun without all the guilt. That's real partying.

PRAYING GOD'S WORD TODAY

You, Lord, have made the path of the righteous like the light of dawn, shining brighter and brighter until midday (Prov. 4:18). Yes, You have made light dawn for the righteous, gladness for the upright in heart. So I will be glad in the Lord today and praise Your holy name (Ps. 97:11–12). What can defeat or depress me when You have redeemed Me?

DAY 42

New Wine

BEFORE YOU BEGIN
Read John 2:6–11

STOP AND CONSIDER
Jesus performed this first sign in Cana of Galilee.
He displayed His glory, and His disciples believed in Him. (v. 11)

John put his faith in Jesus after this miraculous event at the wedding, but not everyone would. What do you think made John believe in Him? What made others not? _____

_____

_____

The wedding guests in Cana found all their stone jars empty and in need of replenishment. In what areas are you feeling particularly empty right now? _____

_____

_____

_____

This miracle performed in the physical realm was meant to reveal something far more glorious in the spiritual realm. Though Jesus certainly met an immediate need at the wedding, the wine represented something of far greater significance.

I believe this new wine is beautifully implied in Ephesians 5:18. Paul wrote, "Don't get drunk with wine, which leads to reckless actions, but be filled with the Spirit." The passage implies that the filling of the Holy Spirit does in full measure what we try to accomplish when we desire to be drunk with wine.

You see, one reason people drink too much wine is because it changes the way they feel and the way they behave. The "new wine" of Christ does the same thing, but His effects are always good. Jesus came to bring the new wine of the Spirit! Something we can drink our fill of without all the negative side effects of wine and the emptiness it leaves behind in the wake of the temporary fix.

Throughout the Old Testament, only handfuls of people had the Holy Spirit in them or upon them because under the old covenant God gave the Spirit for empowerment more than fulfillment. John's Gospel will reveal later that one of Christ's primary purposes for coming and laying down His life was to send the Holy Spirit to us—not just to walk beside us but to dwell in us. At the first revelation of Christ's glory in Cana, they had no idea that the true New Wine was on its way! The Master of our banquet saved the best of the wine for last.

Beloved, do you realize that joy and gladness are among the many gifts and services Christ brought His Holy Spirit to grant? Check it out for yourself. "The fruit of the Spirit is love, joy, peace, patience, kindness, goodness, faith, gentleness, self-control. Against such things there is no law" (Gal. 5:22–23).

Just think! No matter how much you drink of His Spirit, against such things there is no law. Further, the more you drink, the more fully satisfied you are with love, joy, peace, and all sorts of side effects we're so desperate to achieve. To top off the goblet, instead of losing self-control, we gain it. You can't beat a drink like that!

PRAYING GOD'S WORD TODAY

Lord, I am craving joy today—but only the kind that comes from You, the wine that can make my heart glad and my face shine with oil (Ps. 104:15)—the kind that puts more joy in my heart than others have when their grain and new wine abound (Ps. 4:7)—the kind that gleams like a treasure in this clay jar of mine, proving that this extraordinary power comes from God, not from me (2 Cor. 4:7). I need Your joy today, Lord. It's the only kind worth having.

DAY 43

Just the Two of Us

BEFORE YOU BEGIN
Read John 3:16–21

STOP AND CONSIDER

For God loved the world in this way: He gave His One and Only Son,
so that everyone who believes in Him will not perish but have eternal life. (v. 16)

What would be the implications of a God predisposed to despise us and wish us harm?
What is life like for those who are suspicious of the fact that "God loved the world"?

_____

_____

What does God's love for the world imply about our own relationships? What potentially
drastic step could you take to love a person who could easily be considered your enemy?

_____

_____

_____

One of the most astonishing statistical comparisons between the Gospel of John and the three synoptics is how much more God inspired him to tell us about the world. Based on an word count comparison, Matthew mentions the world ten times, Mark five times, and Luke seven times. The Gospel of John? A whopping seventy-three times! In fact, the totality of John's New Testament contributions informing us about the world constitutes almost half the mentions in the entire New Testament. Obviously we will miss a very important concept in John's Gospel if we overlook what he tells us about the world.

Perhaps the most overwhelming is a concept to which we've grown inordinately casual: Jesus was sent by God to the world.

John 17 tells us that the Father and Son had fellowship and shared glory before the world even existed. Jesus said, "Father, glorify Me in Your presence with that glory I had with You before the world existed" (John 17:5). In fact, I am absolutely convinced that mankind exists out of the holy passion of the Trinity to draw others into their fellowship. Thus, the plan of salvation was already completely intact before the creation of the world. Then when the Holy Trinity was ready, each member participated in the creation.

Genesis 1:1: "In the beginning God created the heavens and the earth." Stay with me here. The Word of God delineates between one little planet He called the earth and the entire rest of the universe. We have no idea what is out there. What little science documents and hypothesizes makes Genesis 1:1 inconceivably impressive.

Our solar system is in a galaxy called the Milky Way. Scientists estimate that more than 100 billion galaxies are scattered throughout the visible universe. Astronomers have photographed millions of them through telescopes. The most distant galaxies ever photographed are as far as 10 billion to 13 billion light-years away. The Milky Way's diameter is about 100,000 light-years. The solar system lies about 25,000 light-years from the center of the galaxy. There are about 100 billion stars in the Milky Way.[16] Imagine, 100 billion stars estimated in our galaxy alone, and Psalm 147:4 tells us God "counts the number of the stars; He gives names to all of them."

Impressive, isn't it? In the beginning God created the sun, the moon, every star, all their surrounding planets, and the earth. You and I have no idea what God's activities may have been elsewhere in the universe, but according to the Bible and as far as He wanted us to know, He picked out one tiny speck upon which to build a world. Our world. And He picked it out so that when the time had fully come, He could send His Son (Gal. 4:4).

> Much of the world carries on as if their Creator does not exist. Oh, but He does. Bow down, dear children of God. His love has made you great.

Can you imagine the fellowship of the Trinity on the seventh day? As they rested and looked upon the very good work they had accomplished, one planet had been tended like no other to our knowledge. Perfectly placed in the universe with adequate distance from sun, moon, and stars to sustain human life, it was chosen for divine infiltration.

"For God loved the world." Scripture doesn't tell us He loved the sun, the most impressive of the heavenly bodies we can see. Nor are we told that He loved the stars, even though He knows every one of them by name. John goes out of his way, however, to tell us that God loved the world.

In a universe so vast, so incomprehensible, why does God single out one little planet to love? Beloved, absorb this into the marrow of your bones: because we are on it. As despicable as humanity can be, God loves us. Inconceivably, we are His treasures, His prize creation. He can't help it. He just loves us. So much, in fact, that He did something I, with my comparatively pitiful love for my children, would not do for anyone. He "gave His One and Only Son, so that everyone who believes in Him will not perish but have eternal life" (John 3:16).

Dear one, let it fall afresh. I myself am overcome with emotion. Elohim is so huge; we are so small. Yet the vastness of His love—so high, so wide, so deep, so long—envelops us like the endless universe envelops a crude little planet God first called Earth.

My Amanda was one of the dreamiest, most tenderhearted toddlers you can imagine. I often stooped down to talk to her so I could look her right in those big blue-green eyes. Every time I squatted down to talk to her, she squatted down, too . . . and there we'd be. The gesture was so precious I always had to fight the urge to laugh. I dared not, because she was often very serious about those contemplative moments between the two of us.

Of his God, the psalmist wrote, "Your right hand sustains me; / you stoop down to make me great" (Ps. 18:35 NIV). The Amplified Version says it this way: "Your gentleness and condescension have made me great." I don't think the Scripture applies to us in the modern world's terms of greatness. I think it says of us, "You stoop down and make me significant." Yes, indeed. And when the God of all the universe stoops down and a single child recognizes the tender condescension and bends her knee to stoop as well, the heart of God surges with unbridled emotion. And there they are. Just the two of them.

In what area or attitude of your life does His love invite a change of heart? How has a distrust or disbelief of His love kept you from experiencing the life He wants for you?

_____

_____

_____

_____

_____

PRAYING GOD'S WORD TODAY

When I observe Your heavens, the work of Your fingers, the moon and the stars, which You set in place, what is man that You remember him, the son of man that You look after him? You made him little less than God and crowned him with glory and honor. You made him lord over the works of Your hands; You put everything under his feet: all the sheep and oxen, as well as animals in the wild, birds of the sky, and fish of the sea passing through the currents of the seas. Lord, our Lord, how magnificent is Your name throughout the earth! (Ps. 8:3–9). How magnificent is Your love! _____

_____

_____

_____

_____

_____

_____

_____

_____

_____

DAY 44

It's Just Who He Is

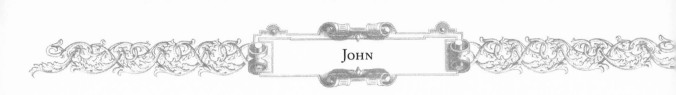
BEFORE YOU BEGIN

Read John 8:48–59

STOP AND CONSIDER

The Jews replied, "You aren't 50 years old yet, and You've seen Abraham?"
Jesus said to them, "I assure you: Before Abraham was, I am." (vv. 57–58)

If the world population were to take a poll on who Jesus is, what statements would likely be among the highest vote-getters? _____

_____

_____

What happens in your heart when you consider that none of their opinions would have one iota of an effect on His identity or His plan for your future? _____

_____

_____

_____

We are going to examine seven claims Christ made in the Gospel of John about who He is. These seven titles are by no means the totality of His claims. They simply share several common denominators in John's Gospel that we don't want to miss. In so doing, we will find that the Gospel of John tells us more about the self-proclaimed identity of Christ than the others. Note Christ's claims of identity in the following Scriptures. No matter how many times you've seen these titles, I pray you will approach them with freshness.

- "I am the bread of life. . . . No one who comes to Me will ever be hungry, and no one who believes in Me will ever be thirsty again." (John 6:35)
- "I am the light of the world. Anyone who follows Me will never walk in the darkness but will have the light of life." (John 8:12)
- "I am the door of the sheep. All who came before Me are thieves and robbers, but the sheep didn't listen to them. I am the door. If anyone enters by Me, he will be saved and will come in and go out and find pasture." (John 10:7–9)
- "I am the good shepherd. The good shepherd lays down his life for the sheep." (John 10:11)
- "I am the resurrection and the life. The one who believes in Me, even if he dies, will live." (John 11:25)
- "I am the way, the truth, and the life. No one comes to the Father except through Me." (John 14:6)
- "I am the vine; you are the branches. The one who remains in Me and I in him produces much fruit, because you can do nothing without Me." (John 15:5).

In fairly rapid succession, Jesus made a point of defining Himself a perfect seven times. I see three basic common denominators in these seven titles. Consider each with me:

1. *All seven titles are preceded by "I am."* I want you to consider the impact of these two words when emitted from the mouth of Jesus the Messiah. That's why I wanted you to look at John 8:48–59 in its entirety, focusing on verse 58, where Jesus said to His accusers, "I assure you: Before Abraham was, I am." The reason they reacted so violently and wanted to stone Him for blasphemy was because they knew exactly what He meant. He was identifying Himself as God. Either Jesus came as the incarnate God, or He is a liar. He cannot be anything in between.

Notice John 18:6, for example. After Judas betrayed Jesus in the garden of Gethsemane, the gathered mob asked Jesus' identity. Christ responded, "I am He," and the entire troop fell backward to the ground. I believe the reason they collapsed before Him is intimated in the original language, where the Greek word for "he" is conspicuously missing. The Interlinear Bible translates it like this: "When He said to them, I AM, they departed into the rear and fell to the ground."

> Every time you discover the reality of Christ fulfilling one of your needs and longings, His name is written on a different part of you.

You see, the rest of us could say "I am," and it would mean nothing more than a common identification. When Christ says the words "I am," they are falling from the lips of Him who is the Great I Am!

2. *The word "the" is included in each title.* Go back and read each of the seven "I am" titles, and you will find in every case Jesus said "I am *the*" rather than "I am *a*." This may seem scholastically elementary, but nothing could be more profound theologically. Just think about your own approach to Jesus Christ. Is He *a* light to you, or *the* Light? Is He *a* way for you to follow—perhaps here and there in life—or is He *the* way you want to go? Is He *a* means to the afterlife in your opinion? In other words, deep down inside do you think that several world religions probably offer a viable way to life after death and Jesus is but one of them? Or is He *the* resurrection and the life?

3. *Each of Christ's seven "I Am" statements in John's Gospel is relational.* Christ is many things. He is truly the Great I Am. He is the Savior of the world. He fulfills numerous titles in the Word of God, but I believe the spiritual implication of the seven "I am" sayings in the broad approach of John's Gospel is this: Jesus Christ is everything we need. Every one of these titles is for us! Remember, He is the self-sufficient One! He came to be what we need—not just what we need but what we desire most in all of life. The "I Am" came to be with us.

We will never have a challenge He can't empower us to meet. We will never have a need He can't fill. We will never have an earthly desire He can't exceed. When we allow Christ to be all He is to us, we find wholeness. One piece at a time. Every time you discover the reality of Christ fulfilling another realm of your needs and longings, His name is written on a different part of you, and you are that much closer to wholeness.

Look back over the seven statements from the previous page. How he has been each of these things in your life? Not just *a*, but *the!* _____

_____

_____

_____

_____

Praying God's Word Today

O Lord, my one desire is to be presented to You as a pure virgin—not one whose mind has been corrupted from a complete and pure devotion to You, the way the serpent deceived Eve by his cunning. O Lord, please forbid that I would ever accept or put up with another Jesus! (2 Cor. 11:2–4). I have asked one thing from You, Lord. This is what I desire: to dwell in Your house all the days of my life, gazing on Your beauty and seeking You in Your temple (Ps. 27:4). May I see You today and always for who You really are. _____

_____

_____

_____

_____

_____

_____

_____

_____

_____

_____

DAY 45

With You or Within You?

Before You Begin

Read John 14:15–18

Stop and Consider

The world is unable to receive Him because it doesn't see Him or know Him.
But you do know Him, because He remains with you and will be in you. (v. 17)

What do you "know" about the Holy Spirit from the Word and from personal experience?
What evidence do you have that He is not only "with you" but is "in you"? _____

_____

_____

Why is this biblical truth so important—so essential, in fact, to our life as a Christian?

_____

_____

_____

_____

Without exception, John's Gospel equips us with more information about the Holy Spirit than any of the synoptics. I wish somehow I could write the next statement in neon lights upon this page to catch the eye of every reader: *The Holy Spirit is the key to everything in the life of the believer in Christ!*

I have testified many times to my defeated Christian life through my teenage years and early twenties, even though I rarely missed a church service or activity. I take full responsibility for my own defeat because I could have read for myself what the churches I attended at those times did not teach me. But although I received many wonderful treasures from the churches of my youth, I did not learn two of the most vital keys to a victorious life: how to have an ongoing, vibrant relationship with God through His Word and how to be filled with the power and life of the Holy Spirit. Both of these are vital concepts that the enemy does everything he can to make us miss. The Word and the Holy Spirit are by far his biggest threats.

One of the most revolutionary truths Christ told His disciples is in John 14:17. He told them that the Spirit of Truth at that time was living *with* them but would soon be *in* them. Think about the repercussions of that promise. What difference could the Spirit of God make living *in* a person as opposed to *with* a person? Beloved, that very difference turned a band of fumbling, fleshly followers into sticks of spiritual dynamite that exploded victoriously on the world scene in the book of Acts. The difference is enormous! Impossible to overestimate! He then filled them in a far more powerful expression at Pentecost in Acts 2:1–4. These glorious events unleashed a new revolutionary economy of the Holy Spirit for the "Church Age" and onward until the return of Christ.

The Holy Spirit now indwells every person who receives Christ as his or her personal Savior (Rom. 8:9). Oh, that we would absorb the magnitude of that spiritual revolution! Dear believer in Christ, the Spirit of the living God—the Spirit of Jesus Christ Himself, the Spirit of Truth—dwells inside of you! Have we heard these concepts so long that we've grown calloused to them?

PRAYING GOD'S WORD TODAY

How wonderful it is, Lord, that what no eye has seen and no ear has heard, and what has never come into a man's heart, is what You have prepared for those who love You. You have revealed these to us by Your Spirit—the One who searches everything, even the deep things of God (1 Cor. 2:9–10). Show me more, Holy Spirit! My eyes, my ears, my heart— my whole being longs to know more of Your love, more of Your power, just more of You!

DAY 46

What Do You Need?

BEFORE YOU BEGIN

Read John 16:5–15

STOP AND CONSIDER

When the Spirit of truth comes, He will guide you into all the truth. . . . He will glorify Me, because He will take from what is Mine and declare it to you. (vv. 13–14)

What do you need from the Lord right now? What is missing in your walk with Him that you've always known could be yours if you really wanted it, if you really asked Him for it?

_____

_____

What do you think would be God's motivation or reasoning for giving you these things?

_____

_____

_____

_____

You and I need nothing on this earth like more of the Holy Spirit. Do we need to love an unlovely person? Do we need extra patience? Could we use a little peace in the midst of chaos? Do we need to show an extra measure of kindness? Could anyone stand a little more faithfulness to God? Could anyone use a strong dose of self-discipline? How about a heaping soulful of joy? Take a look at Galatians 5:22–23. They all come with the fullness of the Holy Spirit! You see, we don't just need more patience. We need more of the Holy Spirit filling us and anointing us!

Now before anybody starts writing me letters, let me go on to explain. I realize the Holy Spirit is a person. When He comes into a believer's life at salvation, He moves in personally. We believers have the Spirit, but the infinite Spirit of God continues to pour Himself into our lives. Any given day I may enjoy a greater portion of His Spirit than I did the day before. He continues to pour out more of His Spirit from on high.

Does anyone need deep insight from God's Word? An added measure of understanding? Anyone need the eyes of her heart enlightened to know the hope of her calling? Does anyone want to fulfill God's eternal purposes for her life and think with the mind of Christ instead of the misleading mind of mortal flesh? All of these come with "more" of the Holy Spirit! (see 1 Cor. 2).

Child of God, don't just absorb this truth! Get up and celebrate it! God gives the Spirit without measure! He has all that you need. Or more properly stated, He *is* all that you need. Our fulfillment and greatest joy are in the flooding of the Holy Spirit of God in our lives. He is how we understand God's Word and will for our lives!

Here's a good one: Could anyone use a sharper memory? Take a look at John 14:26. "The Counselor, the Holy Spirit—the Father will send Him in My name—will teach you all things and remind you of everything I have told you." The Holy Spirit is the blessed Reminder. Have you ever noticed we have a very sharp memory about destructive things but a far duller memory over instructive things? We need more of the Holy Spirit! He is your key to memorizing Scripture or retaining anything biblical. Take Him up on it!

What do you need most from the Holy Spirit? Are you actively praying for more of Him toward that end? Since I began to learn what God made available to me through His Holy Spirit and what He is not only willing but eager to do for me, the level of supernatural power in my life in comparison has skyrocketed. I want the same for you! I am so jealous with a godly jealousy for you that I can hardly stand it!

> The essence of abundant life is an abundance of God in our lives. I don't just want to do the church thing. I want to experience God!

Beloved, every one of these books and Bible studies as well as any message of value God has given me has come directly from the power of the Holy Spirit! I know better than anyone else that I am incapable of any such thing. Years ago I came face-to-face with my own self-destructive humanity, surrendered my life to be crucified with Christ, and determined to live henceforth through the resurrection power of the Holy Spirit. I certainly don't always live my days filled with the Holy Spirit, but the rule (with obvious exceptions) has become the daily pursuit of the Spirit-filled, Christ-empowered life. The difference is night and day. Do I ask for more and more of God's Holy Spirit? You bet I do! And He gives Him without measure! The beauty of His endless supply is that my portion does not take an ounce away from yours!

Now here's a word of warning. Don't confuse asking for more of the Holy Spirit with asking for more manifestations of the Holy Spirit. James 4:2–3 gives us two reasons why we don't receive: We fail to ask, and we ask with wrong motives.

We may not have experienced the fullness of God's presence and empowerment in our lives because we haven't asked. However, sometimes we ask with wrong motives or what the King James Version calls asking "amiss, that ye may consume it upon your lusts." We can have wrong motives for asking for more of the Holy Spirit. Here are a few of my own examples of wrong motives.

• If I want more of the Holy Spirit so that people will be impressed with me or so that I will feel powerful, then my motives are self-glorifying and dishonoring to God.

• If I desire a manifestation of the Holy Spirit as proof that God exists, then my motive is to prove (or to test) God rather than glorify God.

A right motive for asking for more of the Holy Spirit is that God be glorified in you and me through our effective and abundant Spirit-filled lives. Matthew coined it best: "Let your light shine before men, so that they may see your good works and give glory to your Father in heaven" (5:16).

Remember what we learned earlier from John Piper about Christian hedonism? God is most glorified in us when we are most satisfied in Him. Our soul's satisfaction for God's glorification is a wonderful motive for requesting more of the Holy Spirit.

What keeps God's glory from being your chief goal and ambition? What would change in your life if this really became your one desire? _____

_____

_____

_____

_____

_____

_____

Praying God's Word Today

Lord Jesus, You have told us in Your Word that if we, who are evil, know how to give good gifts to our children, how much more will our heavenly Father give the Holy Spirit to those who ask Him? (Luke 11:13). We know this is true, for You have reminded us that You give the Holy Spirit without measure (John 3:34). I need You, Holy Spirit—more and more and more. May You be glorified, even in my request for more of You!

DAY 47

Fruit of the Vine

Before You Begin

Read John 15:1–8

Stop and Consider

My Father is glorified by this: that you produce
much fruit and prove to be My disciples. (v. 8)

What blessings, benefits, and bursts of happiness would be yours if you were to consistently "produce much fruit"? _____

_____

_____

In what way does this "prove" our discipleship? Or, looking at it the other way, what do our examples of fruitlessness prove or reveal about us? _____

_____

_____

_____

What I'm about to say is not to your pastor, your teacher, your mentor, your hero in the faith, your best friend at church, or anyone else. It's to you. Beloved, the God of all the universe has ordained that your precious life bear much fruit.

For several days we've been talking about "more." Now we're going to talk about "much." And I will repeat it as many times as I must. God hasn't appointed you to mediocrity but to a life of profound harvest. I weep for the body of Christ I love so dearly because I am overwhelmed with Paul's godly jealousy (2 Cor. 11:2) that each of you receives, savors, and celebrates what your God has for you.

I am sick of the enemy's subtle scheme to convince the masses in the body of Christ that only a few lives in each generation are truly significant. Your life was set apart for significance! Get up right this second, look in the nearest mirror, and say it out loud to that image in front of you. And while you're at it, say, "God has chosen you, and He wants to be glorified by you bearing much fruit."

I'm not saying another word until you go to that mirror. My friend, sometimes what you and I need is a good fussing at. We are not yet fully believing God! If we were, we'd be so astounded and delighted in Him and living so far beyond ourselves that we wouldn't be able to contain our joy. We somehow continue to entertain those things that hold us back from immensely productive lives.

I hope we clear a few of those obstacles out of the way through the course of this book, but I'd like to address one right away. Many think that the sins of their pasts have exempted them from tremendously fruit-bearing lives. First, if that were true, I assure you I would not be writing to you right now. Second, if we haven't repented and allowed God to restore us and then redeem our failures, we will tragically fulfill some of our own self-destructive prophecies. God is not the one holding us back from "much fruit" after failure. In tandem with the devil, we are the ones. God's primary concern is that He is glorified. Few unmistakable evidences glorify Him more than powerfully restored lives that humbly and authentically proclaim His faithfulness to the death.

Praying God's Word Today

Lord, like the remnant of the house of Judah, I want to take root downward and bear fruit upward (Isa. 37:31), having heard Your Word with an honest and good heart, and by holding on to it—by enduring—to bear much fruit for You (Luke 8:15). Hear my prayer, know my heart, and tend Your garden for Your glory.

DAY 48

How Does
Your Garden Grow?

BEFORE YOU BEGIN
Read John 15:9–17

STOP AND CONSIDER
If you keep My commands you will remain in My love,
just as I have kept My Father's commands and remain in His love. (v. 10)

Why is a constant awareness of God's love for us so vital in a profusely fruit-bearing life?

_____

_____

What have been the costs of trying to bear fruit based on your own human reasoning—
to make things work for God? Why is it so important not to force fruit but to let it grow?

_____

_____

_____

_____

The Father is so adamant that we bear much fruit, He has extended practically inconceivable offers to us. As I share them with you, pardon my excitement as I dangle a few happy participles. He offers to us:

1. *A love we can live in.* When will we get through our heads how loved we are? Take a look at perhaps the most astounding verse in this entire segment of Scripture: "As the Father has loved me, I have also loved you" (John 15:9). Try to grasp this truth as tightly as you can: Christ Jesus loves you like the Father loves Him. He loves you like His only begotten—as if you were the only one! Christ then follows His statement with a command: "Remain in My love." I love the King James word for "remain"—*abide*. The term means exactly what it implies: to dwell in His love, remain in it, tarry in it, soak in it. For heaven's sake, live in it!

Even the most steadfast among God's servants make mistakes and foolish decisions of some kind along the way. We will always give Satan plenty of ammunition to discourage us. But if we don't literally camp in the love of Christ, we will talk ourselves out of untold fruit by dwelling on our own unworthiness. Accept the fact that we are unworthy and yet lavishly loved by a God of redemptive grace.

2. *A source we can draw from.* If we were to list the kinds of things that hold us back from immensely fruit-bearing lives, we might include "a lack of talent or ability." But conspicuously missing in this dissertation on lives bearing much fruit is any reference whatsoever to ability. The one requirement for a profusely fruit-bearing life is that we abide in Christ the same way a branch remains physically attached to the vine. All we have to do is embed ourselves in Him, let the power source flow, and He'll do the work through us. That's the secret! The branch must remain open to the flow of the vine's life. If the branch were simply wound around the vine tightly, it would still die without producing any fruit.

We so often have our own agendas about how we want to serve God. We spend untold energy but never produce lavish and God-glorifying fruit. We have to be open to the power flow and the purposed work the Vine wants to accomplish.

3. *A Gardener we can depend on.* You've heard of personal trainers. Our Gardener is so determined for fruitful lives to bear even more fruit, He commits Himself as their personal pruner! Notice verse 2: "Every branch in Me that does not produce fruit He removes, and He prunes every branch that produces fruit so that it will produce more fruit." I believe this verse suggests that God works all the harder on the child who is producing fruit so she or he will produce even more.

We can't force fruit. If we're going to produce much fruit, we've got to be open to the life, agenda, and timing of the Vine.

If you are a true follower of Jesus Christ, I bet you sometimes feel like God is picking on you. Have you ever exclaimed in exasperation, "God never lets me get away with anything"? Have you ever noticed, though, that God seems particularly jealous with you? That He extracts from your life those mindless and meaningless activities that He seems to "put up with" in other believers' lives? That, dear one, is because you have proved to be a cooperative fruit-bearing child and He knows He has a prime branch through whom He can be all the more glorified.

Do you see the progression suggested in verses 2 and 5? God desires for those who bear fruit to bear *more* fruit—and for those who bear *more* fruit to bear *much* fruit! As nervous as the thought may make us, God can be trusted with a pair of shears in His hand.

4. *Joy we can revel in.* The fact of the matter is that we have been called to lives of obedience. Yes, the grace of God covers our sins as we trust in Christ's finished work on the cross. But we will not bear much fruit without obedience to our Father's will. In fact, according to John 15:10, if we don't walk closely to Him in obedience, we will never draw near enough to abide in His love. He loves us no matter what we do, but we will not be able to pitch our spiritual tents in His presence when we're disobedient. Does all this sound like a life of just serving and sacrificing?

Then you'd better read John 15:11 again. Jesus said, "I have spoken these things to you so that My joy may be in you and your joy may be complete." What an amazing thought! God is sovereign and could have rigged the plan to serve Him only. He could have demanded our obedience and service—or else. He didn't. Our heavenly Father is the giver of all good gifts (James 1:17). God longs to bless us with abundant life and joy. And not just any joy—Christ's joy! Perfect, full, magnetic, and contagious!

The joy of Jesus comes to the believer only one way: transfusion. Like an intravenous drip from Vine to branch! God doesn't just have more for you. He has much. Much love. Much fruit. Much joy. And in the process, the God of the universe derives much glory from one measly mortal. Who can beat a deal like that?

To the best of your biblical understanding, based on an abiding sense of God's presence and pleasure as opposed to numbers and notoriety, where do you think you may presently be on a scale from "no apparent fruit," to "some fruit," then "more fruit," and finally to "much fruit"? What would move you farther along the scale? _____

_____

_____

_____

_____

_____

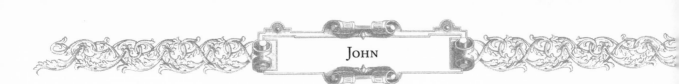

PRAYING GOD'S WORD TODAY

Lord God, You have warned us not to despise Your instruction nor to loathe Your discipline, for You discipline the one You love, just as a father disciplines the son he delights in (Prov. 3:11–12). Prune me to Your heart's content, that my life may bring glory to You.

DAY 49

Talking Points

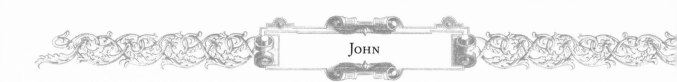
BEFORE YOU BEGIN

Read John 14:19–21

STOP AND CONSIDER

The one who loves Me will be loved by My Father.
I also will love him and will reveal Myself to him. (v. 21)

What are some specific ways that God has revealed Himself to you lately? How have you been tangibly aware of His power, love, and reality? _____

_____

_____

What does the depth of our love for Him have to do with the depth of His revelation to us? How does our devotion invite His presence and communication? _____

_____

_____

_____

God has never revealed Himself to me in flames of fire from within a bush like He did to Moses in Exodus 3:2; nor have I ever seen chariots of fire like Elisha; but I have often beheld God's glory through nature. My soul is as drawn to a certain chain of mountains in the Northwest as a river is drawn to the sea. At least several times a year I feel the wooing of God to come and meet Him there. I confer with Him every day at home, but occasionally our souls crave a display of His glory that can best be seen against a less common backdrop, don't they?

Not too long ago I stayed by myself in a small place in the national park overlooking "my" mountains. Every night when I got into bed, I reminded myself that I had come for rest as well as inspiration. I'd try to talk myself into sleeping past dawn, but I never could. I rose every morning long before light, threw on a heavy coat, and drove to find a front-row seat to behold the sunrise. I rolled down my window to hear the mighty beasts of the field bugle their presence. In perfect covenant consistency, every morning God caused the rays of sunlight to baptize the tips of the mountain—then I watched until He bathed the valley as well. I was so overcome by the majesty such awesomeness suggested that I thought my heart would leap from my chest. At such a moment, Habakkuk 3:3–4 invaded my thoughts:

> His splendor covers the heavens, and the earth is full of His praise.
> His brilliance is like light; rays are flashing from His hand. This is
> where His power is hidden.

God's Word suggests He can reveal Himself in numerous ways, but His ultimate revelation to man was through His very own Son, Jesus. He came to show us God in an embraceable, visible form. I believe a very important part of Christ's promise in John 14:21 is that after His departure, He would continue to reveal, manifest, or make Himself known to His followers through the witness of His Spirit and the power of His Word.

Praying God's Word Today

Lord, You establish the mountains by Your power, robed with strength, so that even those who live far away are awed by Your signs (Ps 65:6, 8). Yet these are but the fringes of Your ways (Job 26:14). I rejoice in the way revealed by Your decrees as much as in all riches. I will meditate on Your precepts and think about Your ways. I will delight in Your statutes; I will not forget Your word (Ps. 119:14–16). May nothing ever delight me as much as Your Son and Your Word. _____

DAY 50

Welcome Home

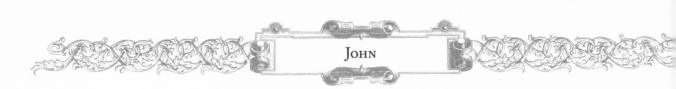
Before You Begin

Read John 14:22–26

Stop and Consider

If anyone loves Me, he will keep My word. My Father will love him,
and We will come to him and make Our home with him. (v. 23)

What kind of "home" are you inviting God into? How are you making Him welcome?

_____

_____

Where do find yourself resistant to His presence? Are there areas of your life or home that are off-limits to openness? _____

_____

_____

_____

_____

One of the most significant qualities found in God's brand of love is that it is demonstrative. Christ directed His followers to love as He loved them. This implies that the more we obey and love God, the more vividly we may see, experience, and enjoy demonstrations of His love. But like His disciples, we are often unable to recognize the demonstration until we obey the wooing of the Spirit in repentance and sprout the firstfruits of love.

I've lived an illustration that might help: God brought a darling young woman into my life who had been through untold turmoil. Abused and misused, she didn't trust anyone. She needed love as badly as anyone I had ever known, but she was terribly suspicious and hard to show love to. God, however, kept insisting that I show her the love of Jesus.

One day I said to Him, "Lord, I'm trying to be obedient, but she is just like trying to hug a porcupine!" Over the months and years, God turned my beloved porcupine into a puppy. I loved her throughout our relationship, but the softer and more loving she became, the more love I was able to show her. As she grew more loving, she could better receive the love I had for her.

On a much greater scale, I believe the principle applies to God's demonstration of love to us. I am convinced that the more we obey and love Christ Jesus, the more He will disclose Himself to us. We are perpetually surrounded by means through which He could show us His worth, His providence, and His presence. But we must open the eyes of our spirit to see it—by loving Him and obeying Him.

I am persuaded that the truth God inspired in the apostle John became the apostle's virtual philosophy and approach to life. We have already concluded that John forsook ambition for affection. Love became his absolute center. He was a man who pursued obedience even when no one was watching. With his whole being, He lived the divine conditions of John 14.

Years down the road, then, is it any wonder our immortal Savior and Lord handpicked him when He determined to deliver the incomparable book of Revelation? How fitting. John himself represents the ultimate human example of his own penmanship.

Praying God's Word Today

Lord, You have proven Your love for us in that, while we were still sinners, Christ died for us (Rom. 5:8). May we, therefore, be imitators of You, as dearly loved children. May we walk in love, as Christ also loved us and gave Himself for us, a sacrificial and fragrant offering to God (Eph. 5:1–2).

DAY 51

Women Allowed

BEFORE YOU BEGIN
Read John 4:27–38

STOP AND CONSIDER

Just then His disciples arrived, and they were amazed that He was talking with a woman. Yet no one said, "What do You want?" or "Why are You talking with her?" (v. 27)

What proof do you have that Jesus made time for, talked to, honored, and treated women with dignity? What does this say about Him? _____

_____

_____

What are a few of the inferiorities some women bring into their Christian experience, even though Christ and His Word promote their value? _____

_____

_____

_____

Hear me clearly: I am pro-men. And (not but) I am also pro-women. What may come as a news flash to some is that these pros are not exclusive. I believe the biblical roles and responsibilities of men and women differ sometimes to complement and complete each other, but our places in the heart of God are the same.

Yes, Jesus speaks to women who listen. Always has. Always will. Anyone who wants to believe Christ didn't have profound encounters with women might want to skip the Gospel of John, because it supplies many detailed accounts that are abundant in meaning.

John 4:1–39, for example, introduces us to the woman from Sychar. You probably know her by the label "the woman at the well," but do you realize she was the first person to whom Jesus declared His messiahship? He led their conversation from His request for a drink to His gift to her of Living Water. The woman then became an evangelist as she returned to Sychar to proclaim: "Come, see a man who told me everything I ever did! Could this be the Messiah?" (John 4:29).

John 8:1–11 tells of the religious leaders grabbing a woman who was taken in the act of adultery and bringing her before the Lord. There they demanded that Jesus judge her, but He refused to play their game. He knelt and drew on the ground until their consciences began to accuse them. When the crowd melted away, Christ asked the woman, "Where are they? Has no one condemned you?" When she replied, "No one, Lord," Jesus responded, "Neither do I condemn you. Go, and from now on do not sin any more" (vv. 10–11).

John 11:17–44 recounts Jesus arriving in Bethany after the death of his friend Lazarus, and we see him dealing with the two sisters, Mary and Martha, as individuals. Martha went to meet Jesus with combined words of reproach and hope. "If You had been here, my brother wouldn't have died. Yet even now I know that whatever You ask from God, God will give You." (vv. 21–22). Jesus calmly accepted her words and revealed Himself to her in a fresh way. "I am the resurrection and the life. The one who believes in Me, even if he dies, will live. Everyone who lives and believes in Me will never die—ever. Do you believe this?" (vv. 25–26).

Mary met Jesus differently. She also stated her belief that Jesus could have healed her brother, but she fell at His feet weeping. In this case Jesus "was deeply moved in spirit and troubled" (v. 33 NIV). He asked where they had laid Lazarus, and Christ wept. Then to the joy of both sisters He called Lazarus from the grave.

John 12:1–8 continues the story of Martha and, particularly, Mary. Six days before the Passover when Jesus would die, the sisters gave a dinner in Jesus' honor. Overcome by her love for Jesus and, I suspect, both motivated by a premonition of what was to come and driven by the Spirit, Mary poured perfume on Jesus' feet and wiped them with her hair. Judas Iscariot declared the gesture an extravagant waste of what could have gone to the poor. But Jesus declared Mary's action sacred in anointing Him for His burial. Matthew 26:13 (NIV) wraps up this scene best with Jesus' words: "I tell you the truth, wherever this gospel is preached throughout the world, what she has done will also be told, in memory of her." Our very words at this moment continue the fulfillment of His promise.

> He replaces every woman's shame with dignity. He brings resurrection life to her loss. He appoints and approves her good works.

Based on these segments—and many others we could list—three things about Christ astound me and make me fall even more in love with Him:

1. *Jesus was not ashamed to be seen with a woman.* This may not seem like a big deal, but how many of us have dated someone or even married someone who seemed ashamed at times to be seen with us? Beloved, Jesus Christ isn't ashamed to be seen with you. In fact, He wants nothing more! He's also not ashamed to talk to you. I meet so many women who are timid about sharing what they've gleaned in Bible study because they don't have much education and they're "probably wrong." Listen, the One who spoke the worlds into being has chosen you for a bride! Study His Word like someone being spoken of and spoken to! He wants your life to radiate proof that He's been talking to you. He's proud of you!

2. *Though very much a man, Jesus understood the needs of a woman.* I despise that ridiculous feminist "theology" that tries to make a woman out of God or at least make Him feminine so we can feel like we have an advocate—"someone who understands." Beloved, Christ understands us better than we do! Of course, He has a decided advantage over every other man. He wove us together in our mother's womb. Still, I'm relieved to know that I am never too needy for Christ—particularly when I'm feeling a tad high maintenance. Did you notice how personal He got in almost every scenario? He was totally unafraid of intimacy then—and He still is.

3. *Without exception, Jesus honored women and gave them dignity.* Do you see a single hint of second-class treatment? In any stretch of the imagination, can you make a woman-hater out of Jesus? Not on your life.

As a woman, you certainly have needs you'd hardly expect a man to understand. But your Jesus knows you intimately—knows your heart, your motivations, your thought processes. You may not be comfortable even writing about such needs in this space, but will you bring them to Him today? I promise you, He longs to hear from you. He loves you so much.

_____

_____

_____

_____

_____

Praying God's Word Today

How can I thank You, Lord, for giving us an advocate with the Father—Jesus Christ the righteous One (1 John 2:1). For we do not have a high priest who is unable to sympathize with our weaknesses, but One who has been tested in every way as we are, yet without sin. Therefore we approach the throne of grace with boldness, so that we may receive mercy and find grace to help us at the proper time (Heb. 4:15–16). We draw near at Your invitation for You to talk with us, hear us, change us. _____

DAY 52

Mine!

Before You Begin

Read John 5:16–23

Stop and Consider

"My Father is still working, and I am working also.". . . Not only was He breaking the Sabbath, but He was even calling God His own Father. (vv. 17–18)

What are some things that you once insisted belonged to you, but God found some very creative ways to show you otherwise? _____

_____

_____

How important is it to know that God is your Father—that although His children are vast and many, you have been singularly chosen by Him for His possession? _____

_____

_____

_____

_____

One of the first passionate words out of a toddler's mouth is, "Mine!" I'm not even sure this word has to be taught. No one will argue where two-year-olds get "No!" but where in the world do they get "Mine"? I'd like to suggest that possessiveness is one of the most intrinsic elements embedded in the human psyche. No one has to learn a "my" orientation. It's intertwined in every stitch of our DNA.

God created us with a need to know that something belongs to us. From the time we are toddlers, we begin testing what is ours by process of elimination. Everything is "mine" until we learn from our parents what doesn't belong to us and what can be taken from us. "No, child, that's not yours, but here's this blanket. It is yours." In fact, perhaps we could say that maturity is not so much disregarding our "my" orientation as learning how to appropriately recognize and handle what is and isn't ours.

I don't know about you, but I need to know that a few things really do belong to me. I am convinced that a certain need to possess is so innate in all of us that if we could truly not call anything our own, our souls would deflate with hopelessness and meaninglessness. Please hear this: ours is not a God who refuses us the right to possess anything. He's simply protective enough of our hearts not to encourage a death grip on things we cannot keep. He's not holding out on us. He's not dangling carrots in front of our noses, then popping us in the mouth when we lunge to bite the bait. Contrary to much public opinion, God is not playing some kind of sick "I-created-you-to-want-but-will-not-let-you-have" game with us. Quite the contrary, the Author of Life will only encourage us to call "mine" what is most excellent. Most exquisite. So to those who receive, God gives Himself.

Part of the human condition means that to live in any semblance of order, we must confront a never-ending influx of "no's." In the midst of so much we cannot have, God says to His children, "Forsake lesser things and have as much as you want of . . . Me." While God is the owner and possessor of all things, He freely invites us to be as possessive over Him as we desire. He is my God. And your God. He's the only thing we can share lavishly without ever decreasing our own supply.

PRAYING GOD'S WORD TODAY

As David once said of You, "I love You, Lord, my strength. The Lord is my rock, my fortress, and my deliverer, my God, my mountain where I seek refuge, my shield and the horn of my salvation, my stronghold" (Ps. 18:1–2). Yes, *my* rock! *My* fortress! *My* deliverer. Thank You, Father, for being mine! _____

DAY 53

Insist on It

BEFORE YOU BEGIN
Read John 13:1–5

STOP AND CONSIDER

Jesus knew that the Father had given everything into His hands,
that He had come from God, and that He was going back to God. (v. 3)

This firm stance of Jesus made certain groups and individuals want to wipe Him off the face of the earth. What biblical stances of yours often draw the consternation of others?

_____

_____

What effect does Jesus' insistence on core truths have on your backbone? What do you think John learned from seeing Jesus walk with freedom and confidence in His identity?

_____

_____

_____

When Christ came to this planet, He forsook many of His intrinsic divine rights in order to accomplish His earthly goals. Philippians 2:7 says he "emptied Himself by assuming the form of a slave, taking on the likeness of men." John 1:3–4 tells us "all things were created through Him, and apart from Him not one thing was created that has been created. Life was in Him, and that life was the light of men." Yet Christ didn't walk around saying, "Hey, bud, do you see that dirt you're walking on? Who do you think made that?"

To our knowledge, Christ didn't sit with the disciples in the moonlight and tout His ownership over the heavens by giving them all the proper names of the stars. In alphabetical order. When we consider that Jesus Christ came to earth as the fullness of the Godhead bodily, He actually showed amazing restraint in exercising His divine rights. Matthew 26:53–54 offers one example. As the mob was arresting Him, He told Peter to put away his sword. "Do you think that I cannot call on My Father, and He will provide Me at once with more than 12 legions of angels? How, then, would the Scriptures be fulfilled that say it must happen this way?"

Jesus made a point of fully exercising one right, however, to the constant chagrin of the Jews. Jesus freely claimed His Sonship to the Father. None of the comparative statistics between Gospels is more staggering than the number of references to God as Father. Approximately 110 times out of 248 references to God as Father in the New Testament occur in the Gospel of John. No other New Testament book comes close.

Never lose sight of the fact that relationship came to mean everything to the apostle John. When you think about John from now on, immediately associate him as one who was wholly convinced of Jesus' love. In turn, John had much to say not only about reciprocal love but love for one another. We will see the concept only swell over the remaining chapters of this book. I don't believe we're off base in assuming that the priority of relationship with Christ is exactly what fitted him to receive the great Revelation.

To John, identity came from association. He very likely absorbed this philosophy from tagging along with Jesus.

Christ knew His constant references to God as His Father incited the Jews riotously, yet He was so insistent, He had to make a point. Through His actions and expressions, Christ seemed to say, "I've set aside My crown, My position, My glory, and soon I'll set aside My life for all of you. But hear me well: I will not lay down my Sonship. God is My Father. Deal with it."

> You will never be required to lay aside your rights of sonship, nor must you ever fall to Satan's temptation to weaken your position.

Dear child of God, if you and I were as unrelenting in exercising our rights of sonship (or daughtership), our lives would be transformed. Satan would never be able to dislodge us from God's plan and blessing. You see, Christ had to make the decision to lay aside many rights, but because He retained the most important one of all, His right of Sonship, Satan could not win. Christ led many sons to glory and got to once again pick up every right He laid aside.

And as those who have received Christ's Spirit of Sonship, the same is true for us. Times may arrive when God asks us to lay down the right to be acknowledged in a situation. Or the right to give our opinion or take up for ourselves. The right to a promotion we think we deserve. The right to leave a spouse even though we might have biblical grounds. The right to withhold fellowship when the other person has earned our distance. The right to be shown as the one who was right in a situation. The right to our dignity in earthly matters. The right to our basic human rights.

But let this truth be engraved on your heart: You will never be required to lay aside your rights of sonship, nor must you ever fall to Satan's temptation to weaken your position. As long as you exercise your rights of sonship, constantly reminding yourself (and your enemy) who God is and who you are, Satan will never be able to defeat you or thwart any part of God's plan for your life. Any loss or other right God permits or persuades you to lay aside is temporary. You will ultimately receive a hundredfold in return.

Hold your position, beloved! Never let anything or anyone talk you out of exercising your rights of sonship! The very reason Satan targets us is because we are the sons (or daughters) of God. He is defeated when we refuse to back off from our positional rights. The last thing he wants to hear from you is, "I am a born-again, justified child of God, and I exercise my right to rebuke you! You, devil, are defeated. You can't take me from my Father nor my Father from me." So, say it!

God will never turn a deaf ear to you or look the other way when you are treated unjustly. As His child, you have 24/7 direct access to Him. You aren't left to "hope" He hears you, loves you, or realizes what's going on. Know it, Sister. Never view your situation in any other context than God as your Father and you as His child.

Are you trying to hold on to all sorts of rights that are completely secondary, yet not exercising the most important right you have—your God-given right of sonship? If you were to defend this right more fiercely, how would it change things in your life? _____

_____

_____

_____

_____

_____

PRAYING GOD'S WORD TODAY

Lord Jesus, You certainly knew times on earth when others were scattered from You, when You were left alone. Yet You declared, "I am not alone, because the Father is with Me" (John 16:32). Your confidence and faithfulness inspire me, Lord, never to receive a spirit of slavery to fall back into fear, but rather to receive the Spirit of adoption, by whom we cry out, "Abba, Father!" (Rom. 8:15–16). I lay claim today—by Your grace—to the rights of family.

DAY 54

Share the Wealth

Before You Begin

Read 1 John 1:1–4

Stop and Consider

What we have seen and heard we also declare to you, so that you may have fellowship along with us . . . with the Father and with His Son Jesus Christ. (v. 3)

How consistent are you in sharing what you've "seen and heard" in Christ? There's more than one way to do this, of course. What opportunities avail you to make Him known?

_____

_____

Try to describe the fellowship you have with others who share your connection to Christ. What thrills your heart about it? What remains missing from it? _____

_____

_____

_____

Years passed. John's beard grayed. The skin once leathered by the sun's reflection off the Sea of Galilee bore the deeper creases of age. His voice rasped the telltale signs of a fiery evangelist. The calluses on his feet became thick with age and country miles. The wrinkles around his eyes folded and unfolded like an accordion as he laughed and mused. While some scholars believe that John's Gospel and his letters were written within just years of one another, few argue that the epistles slipped from the pen of anything other than an aging man. Most believe 1 John was written around AD 85–90.[17]

John had celebrated many Passover meals since the time he leaned his head against the Savior's strong shoulder. So much had happened since that night. He'd never get the picture of Christ's torn frame out of his mind, but neither would he forget his double take of the resurrected Lord. The last time John saw those feet, they were dangling in midair off the tip of the Mount of Olives. Just as quickly, clouds covered them like a cotton blanket. The fire of the Holy Spirit fell . . . then the blaze of persecution seared. One by one the other apostles met their martyrdom. Just as Christ had prophesied, Herod's Temple, one of the wonders of the ancient world, was destroyed in AD 70.

Along the way, the winds of the Spirit had whisked John from all that was familiar— to the city of Ephesus. Decades separated him from those early days of water turned to wine and fishes turned to feasts. For most of us, age means sketchy memories and vague details. Not John. He recorded his clear memories with indelible words. He didn't climb gradually to a pinnacle in writing these epistles. He started at one. His letters seem to open with the mouth of a crescendo as if he had waited until he was about to explode to write it all down. I'm not sure the Holy Spirit as much *fell* on John as *leaped*.

Yes, you would think John's certainty might have waned or weakened with time and distance, but perhaps the most distinguishing mark of a true partaker of the riches of God and Christ is that the partners cannot hoard the treasures. They want everyone else to enjoy them too. Authentic partners and partakers of "fellowship"—*koinonia* in the Greek— simply cannot be selfish. Their joy is only complete as others share in it.

Praying God's Word Today

Lord, I remember a time when John was ordered not to preach or teach at all in Your name. Yet he answered his accusers, "Whether it's right in the sight of God for us to listen to you rather than to God, you decide; for we are unable to stop speaking about what we have seen and heard" (Acts 4:18–20). How I pray that my testimony would be just the same—no matter how long I live—that nothing would ever keep me from declaring Your grace and goodness.

DAY 55

Right Here,
Right Now

Before You Begin

Read 1 John 1:5–10

Stop and Consider

If we confess our sins, He is faithful and righteous to forgive
us our sins and to cleanse us from all unrighteousness. (v. 9)

Like everyone, you certainly have thoughts go through your mind that are harmful to you
and dishonorable to God. How should you and God deal with these? _____

_____

_____

How readily do you receive the forgiveness God promises? What keeps you from living in
an accepted and purified state? _____

_____

_____

_____

First John 1:9 tells us the secrets to sharing a life of fellowshiping with Christ and walking in the light. "If we confess our sins . . ." The basic Greek word for "confession" is *homologeo*, which is derived from two other words. *Homou* means "at the same place or time, together."[18] *Lego* means "to say."[19]

In essence, confession is agreeing with God about our sins. But the portion of the definition that holds the primary key to remaining in *koinonia*—in "fellowship"—is the expediency of "the same place or time." I have confessed and turned from some sins in my life that profoundly interrupted *koinonia*. Why? Because I waited too long to agree with God about them and turn. I still found forgiveness, but *koinonia* was broken through the delay. As God began to teach me to walk more victoriously, I learned to often respond to the conviction of the Holy Spirit at the "same place or time," thereby never leaving the circle of fellowship or the path of "light."

You see, some of us think fellowship with God can only be retained during our "perfect" moments. I want you to see how 1 John 1:8 refutes that philosophy. "If we say, 'We have no sin,' we are deceiving ourselves, and the truth is not in us."

You might ask, "How can a person sin grievously and still remain in fellowship?" Please understand, all sin is equal in its demand for grace, but not all sin is equal in its ramifications (see Ps. 19:13). A person who commits robbery, adultery, or vicious slander departed *koinonia* when he or she refused to agree with God over the sin involved in the thought processes leading up to the physical follow-through. Think of *koinonia* like a circle representing the place of fellowship. We don't just walk in and out of that circle every time a flash of critical thinking bolts through our minds. I don't even think we leave that circle if a sudden greedy, proud, or lustful thought goes through our minds.

If we're in *koinonia* with God, the conviction of the Holy Spirit will come at that "place and time" and tell us those thoughts or initial reactions aren't suitable for the saints of God. Confession without delay not only helps *keep* us in *koinonia*; it is *part of* our *koinonia*!

PRAYING GOD'S WORD TODAY

Lord, how happy is the one whose transgression is forgiven, whose sin is covered! How happy is the man that You do not charge with sin, and in whose spirit is no deceit! When I kept silent, my bones became brittle from my groaning all day long. For day and night Your hand was heavy on me; my strength was drained as in the summer's heat. Then I acknowledged my sin to You and did not conceal my iniquity. I said, "I will confess my transgressions to the Lord," and You took away the guilt of my sin. Therefore let everyone who is faithful pray to You at a time that You may be found (Ps. 32:1–6)—right here, right now. I confess to you the sins of my heart, knowing that remaining in fellowship with You is of more value than any perceived pleasure or desire.

DAY 56

One Thing
You Need to Know

Before You Begin
Read 1 John 3:1–3

Stop and Consider

Look at how great a love the Father has given us, that we should be called God's children. And we are! The reason the world does not know us is that it didn't know Him. (v. 1)

What do you find the hardest to believe about God's level of love for you? How much stock are you genuinely able to place in the verse above? _____

_____

_____

If His love is difficult for you to accept or receive, what do you think might be the cause of your resistance or suspicion? _____

_____

_____

One of our greatest needs as we try to live sanely in our tornadic culture is simplicity—surrendering ourselves to the "one thing" that ensures everything else of great value. We see a perfect example of this concept in the apostle John. As the "disciple Jesus loved," John chose to believe and fully receive the love of Christ above all other things. What was the result? Just as Solomon asked for wisdom and became the wisest man in history, John prioritized love and became a flooding wellspring of affection. When God esteems our prayers, we get what we asked and far more.

I originally learned 1 John 3:1 in the King James Version: "Behold, what manner of love the Father has bestowed upon us." Keep in mind that all the major Bible translations still trace back to the Greek for accuracy. By using the word "behold," I think the apostle John was saying, "Can't you see it? Don't you perceive it? The love of God surrounds us with evidences! Just look!"

If we asked God to help us more accurately grasp the true disposition, character, and exquisite quality of His love for us, our lives would dramatically change! Because John chose to prioritize love, God opened his eyes to behold it and his soul to perceive it. Paul discovered something similar and prayed for all of us to do likewise. His prayer thrills me that we might "know this love that surpasses knowledge" (Eph. 3:19 NIV). I think Paul wanted us to experience God's love to the full measure of our capacity through the Spirit of God within us, then try to comprehend that its true measure and nature are far beyond that very experience. Just a taste. Just a glimpse. We are invited to know a love that is beyond human knowledge.

Beloved, God's love for you exceeds all reason—yes, His love *for you!* First John 4:16 (NIV) says, "We know and rely on the love God has for us." The word for "know" in this verse is the same one Paul employed in Ephesians 3:19. You see, we can't define God's love, but we can behold it, experience it, and rely on it. Is 1 John 4:16 a reality for you? His love for you and me is an absolute reality, *but*—we can be so emotionally unhealthy that we refuse to experience it and absorb it into our hearts and minds.

First John 3:19–20 (NIV) is powerful in this regard: "This then is how we know that we belong to the truth, and how we set our hearts at rest in his presence whenever our hearts condemn us. For God is greater than our hearts, and he knows everything." Ironically, many people are resistant to God because they imagine Him to be very condemning. In reality, humans are *far* more condemning and often emotionally dangerous. I am intrigued by a statement about Christ recorded in John 2:24 (NIV): "Jesus would not entrust himself to them, for he knew all men."

> Satan neither wants us to know who we could be nor what we could do. Lives full of God's power, love, and soundness of mind are a threat to the kingdom of hell.

I can almost imagine Christ saying to humanity, "I am perplexed with all your talk about whether or not you can trust Me. Actually, your heart can be at complete rest in My presence. My love is perfectly healthy. The greater risk is in My entrusting Myself to you." You see, our unhealthy hearts not only condemn us; they condemn others. I have seen marriages destroyed because one spouse refused to accept the reality of the other spouse's love for him or her. Our hearts sometimes even condemn God as we decide for ourselves that He can't be trusted and that He doesn't really love us unconditionally. Our natural hearts are very deceitful and destructive on their own.

I have had the privilege of getting to know many believers over the course of this ministry. And based on what I've seen, I am convinced that few people possess a virtually whole heart who have not pursued it deliberately in Christ. We don't have to be raised in severely dysfunctional homes to develop unhealthy hearts. All we have to do is expose ourselves to life. Life can be heartless and mean. Purely and simply, life hurts. We can't check ourselves out of life, however. Instead, God hopes that we'll turn to Him to heal us from the ravages of natural life and make us healthy ambassadors of abundant life in an unhealthy world.

Please know that God can heal your heart no matter what got it in such a condition. First John 3:20 tells us that God is greater than our hearts! And He knows everything! Yet knowing all things, God loves us lavishly. Perfectly. Unfailingly. If He can heal my shattered, self-destructive heart, He can heal anyone's.

Beloved, Satan is a liar! He knows if you and I take this thing about God's love seriously, we might become a John or a Paul in our generations. Oh, let's glorify God, spite the devil, and do it! It's not too late. Take your pulse. If your heart is still beating, it's worth healing! Here's the catch, however: God's method of healing a condemning heart is to love it to death . . . then create in us a new heart. A healthier heart. A heart filled with faith instead of fear. His perfect love is the only thing that will drive out that fear of ours.

Knowing that "perfect love" is the only thing that "drives out fear" (1 John 4:18), please allow me to ask a very personal question. At this season of your life, deep down in your heart, what things are you most afraid of? What is most in need of His "perfect love"?

PRAYING GOD'S WORD TODAY

Who is a God like you, who pardons sin and forgives the transgression of the remnant of Your inheritance? You do not stay angry forever but delight to show mercy (Micah 7:18). By Your grace, dear Lord, I choose to receive Your lavish, unreasonable, unfailing love— all the way into my marrow.

DAY 57

Otherly Love

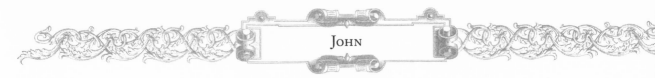
BEFORE YOU BEGIN

Read 1 John 4:7–12

STOP AND CONSIDER

No one has ever seen God. If we love one another,
God remains in us and His love is perfected in us. (v. 12)

We might say we're being called by God to "love difficult people," when in reality we're being challenged to "love people we find difficult." What's the difference? _____

_____

_____

How many people would you estimate you've been very challenged to love in the last five years? What's been the result of these tough relationships? _____

_____

_____

_____

Somehow I don't find loving God quite as challenging as loving a few others I've known. I fear they'd say the same thing. It's with good reason that "Oh, brother!" is a common figure of speech for frustration. Our most serious challenges are usually not with circumstances. They're with people.

But exercising and strengthening the weak muscles of what I'll call "otherly affection" is paramount to God. If I may be simplistic, it's why we're still here. So what's a believer to do with all the challenges to love people we find difficult? Forget faking it. You and I are called to the real thing. While loving others God places in our paths will never cease to be challenging, the key is learning to draw from the resource of God's own *agapao* rather than our own small and selfish supply of natural *phileo* or fondness. *Agapao* is many things we imagine as love, but two primary elements set it apart.

Agapao begins with the will. It is volitional love. In other words, the beginning of true love is the willful decision to agree with God about that person and choose to love. Secondly, when Scripture makes a distinction between *agapao* and *phileo*, *agapao* love is based on best interest while *phileo* love is based on common interests. *Phileo* love often originates through preference and taste, as in a naturally developed friendship or sisterly relationship. *Agapao* tends to be the more "expensive" love because the element of sacrifice is part of its nature. It's simply harder. It necessitates will over emotion.

God's chief goal is to deepen each of our relationships with Him. And He knows that if we don't see our need for Him, we will never understand how sufficient and wonderful He is. Therefore, He continually challenges us to live beyond our natural abilities. He knows that challenges like loving someone we find difficult will place the obedient in the position to come to Him constantly for a fresh supply of His love. We have to pour out our own toxic and preferential affections so our hearts can be filled with His affections. As we ask for our cups to overflow with *agapao*, the liquid, living love of God will not only surge through our own hearts; it will splash on anyone nearby. Glory!

Praying God's Word Today

O Lord, Your love has been poured out in my heart through the Holy Spirit You have given me (Rom. 5:5). But if I see a brother in need and shut off my compassion from him—how can I say that Your love resides in me? (1 John 3:17). Lord, help my love to be sincere and without hypocrisy (Rom. 12:9), to love my enemies, to do what is good, expecting nothing in return. This will confirm in my heart that I am a child of the Most High, for You are certainly gracious to the ungrateful (Luke 6:35).

DAY 58

Straying Lambs

BEFORE YOU BEGIN
Read 1 John 4:20–5:5

STOP AND CONSIDER

Everyone who believes that Jesus is the Messiah has been born of God,
and everyone who loves the parent also loves his child. (v. 1)

Do you know of any spiritual castaways in your church? In your family? What could you and others from your body do to restore these ones to fellowship with Christ? _____

_____

_____

To what lengths should this kind of restorative love go? Are there limits to how much mercy we should extend or how much effort we should make to bring others back? _____

_____

_____

_____

My favorite account from the early church fathers concerning John was preserved by Clement. It begins with the statement, "Listen to a story which is not a story but a true tradition of John the Apostle preserved in memory."

While visiting a new bishop and his congregation in Smyrna, John "saw a young man of strong body, beautiful appearance, and warm heart. 'I commend this man to you,' [John] said, 'with all diligence in the face of the church, and with Christ as my witness.'"

John returned to Ephesus and, as promised, the bishop took the young man under his wing and baptized him. Time passed, and the bishop "relaxed his great care and watch-fulness. . . . But some idle and dissolute youths, familiar with evil, corrupted him in his premature freedom." Before long, the young man had given himself entirely to a life of sin, committed crimes, and even renounced his salvation. Eventually John was summoned back to Smyrna and asked for a report of the young man. Somewhat taken aback, the bishop answered, "He has died"—meaning he had abandoned his faith.

John replied, "Well, it was a fine guardian whom I left for the soul of our brother. But let me have a horse, and someone to show me the way." When the elderly John found the young man, he started to flee. John called out to him, "Why do you run away from me, child, your own father, unarmed and old? Pity me, child, do not fear me! You have still hope of life. I will account to Christ for you. If it must be, I will willingly suffer your death, as the Lord suffered for us; for your life, I will give my own. Stay, believe; Christ sent me." (John knew better than anyone else that only Christ could ransom a man's life.)

The young man wept bitterly, embraced the old man, and pleaded for forgiveness. The account says that John led the young man back and "baptized him a second time in his tears. . . . He brought him to the church, he prayed with many supplications, he joined with him in the struggle of continuous fasting, he worked on his mind by various addresses and did not leave him, so they say, until he restored him to the church, and thus gave a great example of true repentance and a great testimony of regeneration, the trophy of a visible resurrection."[20] Truly, John practiced what he preached.

Praying God's Word Today

Father, I am drawn by Your Word which says, "If any among you strays from the truth, and someone turns him back, he should know that whoever turns a sinner from the error of his way will save his life from death and cover a multitude of sins" (James 5:19–20). Make me this kind of seeker, Lord—one who searches for the stray (Matt. 18:12). _____

_____

_____

_____

_____

_____

_____

_____

_____

_____

_____

_____

_____

DAY 59

Microscope Days

BEFORE YOU BEGIN
Read 2 John 1–6

STOP AND CONSIDER

To the elect lady and her children, whom I love in truth . . .
because of the truth that remains in us and will be with us forever. (vv. 1–2)

What are some of the absolute truths you know about God—things you can ask the Holy
Spirit to remind you of on days when truth is hard to decipher? _____

_____

_____

What makes truth more reliable than anything else? _____

_____

_____

_____

_____

Most days of the year, I can look at my life through a telescope and sit in utter amazement. God has fulfilled dreams I couldn't have had sense enough to dream. He delivered me from a life of recycling defeat and deeply embedded bitterness. He saved my marriage. He has allowed a former pit-dweller like me to serve someone like you. Oh, He has been indescribably gracious to me . . . just as He has to you.

But then I have these microscope days—days when I am determined to slap the most upsetting thing I can think about on a slide and stare at it for hours, to throw a pity party and resent any loved one who refuses to come.

Let me warn you, Satan will rarely refuse to attend a good pity party. Don't think for a moment that Satan won't confront you on the "day of [your] disaster" (Ps. 18:18 NIV)—whatever that may be. Sometimes we give him credit for having a heart and respecting when something should be off limits. After all, fair fighters don't hit a person when she's down.

Satan is not a fair fighter. He confronts us on our worst days and approaches us with his specialty: lies. You can't imagine the lies he tries to tell me on my microscope days. Other times he tries a different approach. But just about the time I want to default back to my old coldness, the Spirit of God within me whispers warm breath upon my cooling heart.

Many of us have been loved by unhealthy people who proved deceptive in other ways. We were left injured and confused. Incidentally, if we didn't let God heal us, we likely became unhealthy people ourselves who continued the process. Unhealthiness is contagious, and deceived people deceive people.

But truth sets us free. God, the great I Am, is the totality of wholeness, completeness, and self-existence. He is both truth and love! While Satan approaches us with hate and lies, we can be "loved in the truth" by God and by those His Spirit fills. Our God will only tell us the truth, and one of His chief truths is that loving is always worth doing.

I feel much better. Sometimes I just have to talk it out. I'm ready to put up my microscope and go back to my bifocals.

PRAYING GOD'S WORD TODAY

I stand here today, Lord, with truth like a belt around my waist (Eph. 6:14), having puri-fied myself for sincere love of the brothers by obedience to the truth, loving one another earnestly from a pure heart (1 Pet. 1:22). May You get my mind ready for action, being self-disciplined, and setting my hope completely on the grace to be brought to us at the revelation of Jesus Christ (1 Pet. 1:13). My desire is live freely, to love sincerely, to walk at all times in Your truth.

DAY 60

Spiritually Speaking

BEFORE YOU BEGIN

Read 2 John 7–13

STOP AND CONSIDER

Watch yourselves so that you don't lose what we have
worked for, but you may receive a full reward. (v. 8)

What are some of the most prevalent false teachings in our culture today? Which ones do
you most commonly find sneaking their way into your church?_____

_____

_____

How does John tell us to deal with these? How do *you* deal with them? How do you guard
your church and your family from them? _____

_____

_____

_____

No sooner does God reveal truth than Satan goes on the warpath with lies. Deception is his specialty, and his obvious goal is to get us to believe the lies. Therefore, they can't be blatant or we'd recognize them.

Notice John said nothing in this passage about these false teachers refuting every single doctrine concerning Christianity. Some of the false teachers in John's day did not refute that Jesus was divine, for instance. They simply said He wasn't man as well as God. John focused on this exact false teaching in his first letter: "Every spirit who confesses that Jesus Christ has come in the flesh is from God. But every spirit who does not confess Jesus is not from God." (1 John 4:2–3). The issue of Christ coming in the flesh is so vital because we "enter the Most Holy Place by the blood of Jesus, by a new and living way opened for us through the curtain, that is, his body" (Heb. 10:19–20 NIV). Satan is ever trying to undermine the issue of salvation.

Think about this with me. God created man in His image. John 4:24 says, "God is spirit." You and I were created in three parts: body, soul, and spirit. I believe the "spirit" part of us is that which is created most pointedly in God's image. The spirit—when distinguished in Scripture from the soul—is the part of each human being that has the capacity to know and have a relationship with God. Our Maker literally equipped us with an inner longing to find Him.

First Corinthians 6:17 says that "anyone joined to the Lord is one spirit with Him." When we receive Jesus as our Savior, our spirit (that part of us with the capacity to know God) unites with the Holy Spirit, and they become one. So because I am a believer in Christ, when I refer to the spirit within me, I am talking about the Holy Spirit. But Satan wants to do anything he can to keep people blinded to the truth and lost. He knows all of us are created with a longing for God that we often confuse with a longing for anything "spiritual." But not every spiritual teaching is Christian, and he knows it.

The good news of Jesus Christ was running rampant all over the Middle Eastern part of the world in John's day and heading north, south, east, and west. Jesus was a hot topic of conversation. Once Satan established that he couldn't squelch spiritual hunger or stop the talk about Christ, he determined to supply a new story that made best use of both. He suggested through false teachers that Christ indeed came but not in the flesh. Therefore, the spiritually hungry could still have a belief system involving God but remain, as my relatives would say, as lost as a goose. Why? Because our access to God is through the torn flesh of Jesus Christ. To deny the incarnation is to deny the one and only means of salvation.

Do you see what Satan has done? He has tried to feed their need for the spiritual and still keep them blind to the truth.

I imagine you know someone at work or elsewhere that may be very "spiritual" but doesn't believe in the incarnate death of Christ as the means to salvation. Do you see what Satan has done? He has tried to feed their need for the spiritual and still keep them blind to the truth. Clever and terribly destructive, isn't he? Don't judge them. Pray like mad for them! Pray for the veil to be removed and the torn veil of Jesus' flesh to be made clear! Just take note that this is Satan at work.

John warned "the chosen lady" not to take any such teacher into her house. In those days, of course, most gatherings of believers met in what we now call "house churches." In many countries they still do. Though John's directive is certainly important for any individual believer, you can imagine how vital it would be for an entire church gathering. Traveling teachers were very common. I think John was saying, "Don't even consider giving anyone who teaches such false doctrine freedom to speak in your gatherings!"

Recently I spoke in a denominational church I haven't often had the privilege to serve. The pastor stood in the back of the sanctuary and listened to every word I taught. Someone asked me if I was bothered by his presence. I assured them I had nothing but respect for a pastor who watched over his flock so carefully. I also was quite relieved when I passed his test!

Pastors aren't just the shepherds of the men of the church. I have met pastors who I could tell were totally unconcerned about what their women were studying or to whom they were listening. Some of them think we're all just sipping tea and talking girl talk. I find myself thinking, "Mister, with all due respect, if your women catch a fire of false doctrine, they can burn down your whole church! Watch who you take into your "house." Watch *me*, for heaven's sake! Watch all of us!" Many would never knowingly teach deception or distortion, but all are dreadfully human.

Well, well, well. In his second letter John certainly said volumes in so few words. If only I could do the same. One of the things I like best about him is his balance. "Love one another!" And while you're at it, "Test the spirits!" Now that's a fine teacher.

Even in his old age, John sounds like he could go all "Son of Thunder" on those who misrepresented the claims of Christ. What are the great challenges of this in our age of hyper-sensitivity and tolerance? _____

_____

_____

_____

_____

_____

_____

Praying God's Word Today

O Lord, I know that there are false teachers even in our churches today. They secretly bring in destructive heresies, denying the Master who bought them, bringing swift destruction on themselves. But many follow their unrestrained ways, and because of them the way of truth is blasphemed. They exploit people with deceptive words. I know that their condemnation, pronounced long ago, is not idle, and their destruction does not sleep (2 Pet. 2:1–3). In the meantime, though, I pray for the protection of hearts, minds, and spirits, for the purity of Your church, and even for those who preach these false doctrines, that they may see the truth and repent, that none would be deceived. _____

DAY 61

Your All-Around
Health

BEFORE YOU BEGIN
Read 3 John 1–4

STOP AND CONSIDER

Dear friend, I pray that you may prosper in every way
and be in good health, just as your soul prospers. (v. 2)

What role does good health play in the condition of your soul and your relationship with God? Or the other way around—how does your soul's fitness affect you physically? _____

_____

_____

What could Satan do, though, if we become overly fretful about our physical health and the other stresses of age avoidance? What's the balance here? _____

_____

_____

_____

God has taught me serious lessons about the impact my physical body has on both my soul and my spirit. Think about the soul for a moment. If my body is completely exhausted, my soul is deeply affected and over time can absorb the physical weariness and translate it into depression or feelings of hopelessness. If we eat poorly, we can fuel anxiety and fear. Most of us know that stress is linked to heart problems, high blood pressure, and many digestive problems. As long as our souls and spirits are imprisoned in these physical bodies, they are greatly affected by their condition.

You and I live stressful lives. I've heard many of your testimonies, and I am astounded at some of your challenges. Some of you work all day, then tend a sick loved one all night. Others of you hold down several jobs as you try to keep your children in college. I often hear from young mothers who have three or four children under five years old. Now that's stress! I can't even imagine some of your challenges. I never dreamed I would have the challenges I face today. I am so grateful and humbled by God's present calling on my life to minister to women, but I will not kid you. It is work! Yes, God does most of it all by Himself, but the little He requires from me is everything I've got!

My dear co-laborer, you and I cannot effectively fulfill our callings if we don't watch after our health. Our bodies are temples of the Holy Spirit. Each of us faces a life beyond our natural capabilities. My calendar is overwhelming, and I take each scheduled date very seriously. If I end up with a virus and can't make a conference that was scheduled a year earlier, I am devastated. If I'm going to be faithful to you, I've got to cooperate with God and do my part.

Listen, we live in a hard world. That's why I'm convinced that one of our severest needs is pure rest. Not only sleep, but refreshment and recreation. So if you have guts enough not to disconnect and hide from the overwhelming needs out there, you need to add some Sabbath moments into your life to help you keep your head on straight. Start taking them! Hear me, dear friend—"I pray that you may prosper in every way and be in good health, just as your soul prospers."

Praying God's Word Today

Lord, You have taught us in Your Word not to consider ourselves as wise but to fear You and turn away from evil, for this will be healing for our bodies and strengthening for our bones (Prov. 3:8). You have also said that paying attention to Your Word and teaching, keeping them within our heart, will be life to those of us who find them and health to our whole body (Prov. 4:20–22). I receive this today as both a warning and a blessing, wanting to honor You in every part of my life, knowing that You have created me to be whole and healthy and to prosper.

DAY 62

Used in a Sentence

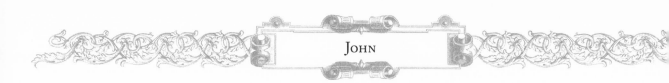

BEFORE YOU BEGIN
Read 3 John 5–14

STOP AND CONSIDER

I wrote something to the church, but Diotrephes,
who loves to have first place among them, does not receive us. (v. 9)

If just one sentence was to be written about your life in Scripture—like this one about Diotrephes—what do you suppose it would be? _____

_____

_____

What would you want it to be? _____

_____

_____

_____

_____

John drops several names in this one-chapter letter of his. Gaius appears as John's dear friend. Diotrephes is seen as one who loved to be first and excluded others. Demetrius bears a good name so that not only others but even the truth speaks well of him.

Imagine being named in a letter that turned out to be inspired Scripture for all the world to see! Whether in commendation or criticism, having your name immortalized in Scripture is a heavy thought!

When I see a portion of Scripture with brief testimonials, I almost shiver. A number of times in my life, I would have been anywhere from devastated to humiliated over what might have been written in a one-sentence statement about my life. That's why I love knowing that as long as we're kicking and breathing, we can still change our testimonies. God hasn't put a period at the end of our sentences yet.

But take note: that tiny little dot doesn't take long to jot. We may think we're only mid-sentence when we're not. Attending as many funerals as I do is a constant reminder to me. Let's not put off working toward what we hope God's testimonial for our lives will state. As the writer of Hebrews said, "Today, if you hear His voice, do not harden your hearts as in the rebellion" (3:15).

Like poor Diotrephes. You'd think with a name like that, he wouldn't have wanted to be first. Can you imagine such a one-sentence testimonial? "Beth loved to be first and didn't like to have anything to do with the common folks." Egads! The hair on the back of my neck is standing up!

Notice John didn't say the man was lost, however. Diotrephes was obviously a member of the church. Though his actions weren't loving, he could easily have been a Christian. Let's admit, if gossip and divisiveness are unquestionable signs of "lostness," the few folks who do go to heaven are liable to have considerable elbow room.

Thank goodness we won't have hard feelings and conflict in glory. Otherwise, I could almost imagine Diotrephes saying to John, "Did you have to go and write it down? Why couldn't you have just gossiped like I did?"

Praying God's Word Today

Lord, there are many things that could be said in testimony about me—some good, some not-so-good. Some true, some misunderstood. But I am so glad that You inspired John to write, "If we accept the testimony of men, God's testimony is greater, because it is God's testimony that He has given about His Son" (1 John 5:9). The story of my life is that You are my life. Help me remember that my life is a testimony about You, not me.

DAY 63

God of Wonders

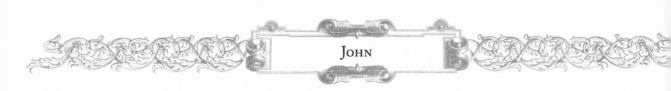
BEFORE YOU BEGIN

Read Revelation 1:1–3

STOP AND CONSIDER

The revelation of Jesus Christ that God gave Him to show His slaves what must quickly take place. He sent it and signified it through His angel to His slave John. (v. 1)

Where is one of the most remote, abandoned places you've ever been—whether physically, emotionally, or spiritually? _____

_____

_____

Did God meet you in this place? How did He do it, and what did you learn from Him?

_____

_____

_____

_____

For the remainder of our journey together, we will join John in exile on the island of Patmos in the Aegean. Don't bother packing your swimsuit. This six-mile-wide, ten-mile-long island is not exactly paradise. In John's day its rocky, barren terrain attracted the eye of the Romans as a perfect place to banish criminals. Under the rule of the Roman emperor Domitian (AD 81–96), Christianity was a criminal offense, and the apostle John had a fierce case of it.

I am curious why John, an undeniable Son of Thunder, was exiled rather than killed under the authority of Roman rule like the other apostles. Scholars agree we can assume he was harshly treated—even at his age—and forced into hard labor in the mines and quarries on the island. I still wonder why the Romans bothered since they publicly and inhumanely took the lives of so many other Christians. Ultimately, God wasn't finished with John's work on earth, and no one was taking him without his Father's permission. I wonder if the traditional teaching of the early church fathers is accurate—that the Romans tried to kill him . . . and couldn't.

In a work called *On Prescription against Heretics*, Tertullian—often called the "father of Latin theology"—made a stunning claim: "The apostle John was first plunged, unhurt, into boiling oil, and then remitted to his island exile!"[21]

Very few scholars question the reliability of the early traditions held about Peter's death on a cross to which Tertullian referred. Likewise, I've never read a commentary that cited reason to question the traditional information that Paul was beheaded like John the Baptist. I certainly don't know if the account regarding John's plunge into boiling oil is reliable, but if you ask me if such an event is possible, I could only answer yes! In Acts 12, God wasn't ready for Peter's work on earth to end, so He loosed his chains and caused him to walk right out of the prison. I can't even count the times the apostle Paul narrowly escaped death. I seem to recall a trio in the Old Testament who experienced fire without even the smell of smoke (see Dan. 3). Beloved, don't let the modern church make you cynical. Ours is a God of wonders, and don't you forget it!

Praying God's Word Today

What god is great like our God? You are the God who works wonders; You have revealed Your strength among the peoples (Ps. 77:13–14) and have made a name for Yourself that endures to this day (Neh. 9:10). Ah, Lord God! You Yourself made the heavens and earth by Your great power and with Your outstretched arm. Nothing—nothing—is too difficult for You! (Jer. 32:17). Even in my remote and darkened places, may I remember that You are God . . . and You can do anything!

DAY 64

Listening Alone

BEFORE YOU BEGIN

Read Revelation 1:4–11

STOP AND CONSIDER

John, your brother and partner in the tribulation, kingdom, and perseverance in Jesus, was on the island called Patmos because of God's word and the testimony about Jesus. (v. 9)

Revelation has many themes, but among its most important is the issue of perseverance and—its blessed companion—hope. Where do you need to see hope the most right now?

_____

_____

What has been your "testimony about Jesus" in recent days? Who needs to hear what the Lord has been revealing to you? _____

_____

_____

_____

We can be quite sure that John never sketched Patmos on his personal itinerary. I wonder what the old man felt as he was shipped like a criminal from his loved ones in Ephesus to a remote, unfriendly island. He had no idea what awaited him. God's ways are so peculiar at times. Yet the greatest privilege of John's life waited for him in these gravest of circumstances.

The most profound revelation in Revelation is the revealing of Jesus Christ Himself, not only in visions but in authority. The word "revelation" (meaning "unveiling") is translated from the Greek word *apokalupsis*. Thrown onto a boat transferring criminals, John had no idea what God would "unveil" to him upon the island of Patmos.

Imagine John's frail, aging frame as he held on tight while the sea vessel tossed its long way across the Aegean. John probably pushed his gray hair out of his face to look at the few other prisoners sharing his destination. Don't picture a bonding experience. No one would likely carry him through a small group of worshipers while he said, "Dear children, love one another." Exile was intended not only for overwork and overexposure to elements; it was purposed for crazing isolation. Yet the tactic would be wasted on John—just as it can be wasted on us when Satan tries to force us into isolation.

John most likely would have preferred death. His long life may have frustrated him. If forced to remain on earth, exile from ministry and isolation from those he loved was certainly not the way he envisioned spending his senior years. I can't imagine at one point or another in the labors forced upon him that John didn't slip on the jagged, rocky surfaces and rip his thinning skin like paper. He had no bedding for his aching body at the end of a day.

I also can't imagine that he thought, "Finally! A little peace and quiet for writing a new book!" He couldn't have expected to meet Jesus on that island as he did. Beloved one, how many testimonies do we need to hear before we accept that sometimes the places and seasons we expect Jesus least, we find Him most? And oddly, sometimes the places we expect Him most, we find Him least.

Yes, when Christ returns to this groaning soil in His glorious splendor, every eye will see Him. But until then, He sometimes comes with clouds. God's glory is so inconceivably brilliant to the human eye that He often shrouds His presence in a cloud (see Exod. 16:10; 24:15–16; Lev. 16:2; 1 Kings 8:10; Luke 9:34). But one day, as Revelation 1:7 says, the clouds will roll back like a scroll and Christ will stand before us revealed.

> How many testimonies do we need to hear before we accept that sometimes the places and seasons we expect Jesus least, we find Him most?

He has much to disclose to us in the meantime, and we'll be greatly helped when we accept that clouds are not signs of His absence. Indeed, within them we most often find His presence. In the July 29 entry of his classic devotional *My Utmost for His Highest*, Oswald Chambers wrote figuratively of clouds:

In the Bible, clouds are always associated with God. Clouds are the sorrows, sufferings, or providential circumstances, within or without our personal lives, which actually seem to contradict the sovereignty of God. Yet it is through these very clouds that the Spirit of God is teaching us how to walk by faith. If there were never any clouds in our lives, we would have no faith. "The clouds are the dust of His feet" (Nahum 1:3). They are a sign that God is there. . . . Through every cloud He brings our way, He wants us to unlearn something. His purpose in using the cloud is to simplify our beliefs until our relationship with Him is exactly like that of a child—a relationship simply between God and our own souls, and where other people are but shadows. . . . Until we can come face-to-face with the deepest, darkest fact of life without damaging our view of God's character, we do not yet know Him.[22]

I've been on Patmos myself when the clouds that settled on the island obscured what might otherwise have been a beautiful view. I wonder if clouds covered the island when Domitian thought he left John to the island's harsh volcanic mercy? I wonder how the old apostle "viewed" his circumstances? I wonder if he ever imagined getting off that island? Or what he'd see while he was there?

John had a critical decision to make while exiled on the unkind island. Would he relax his walk with God at the very least and at most resist? After all, no one from his church or ministry was watching. Would he lie down and die? Goodness knows he was weary. Or would John the Beloved love Christ all the more and seek Him with his whole heart amid the rock and wasteland?

His answer rises like a fresh morning tide baptizing the jagged shore: "I was in the Spirit on the Lord's day" (1:10). And there He was: the Alpha and Omega. The first and last Word on every life. Every trial. Every exile.

Is your life covered in dark clouds right now? Or perhaps the clouds aren't dark. They are simply obscuring clarity and tempting you to be confused by your circumstances. What will you do while waiting for the clouds to part? Is there anyone else who might need your encouragement to stand strong in such stormy conditions? How can you help them? ———

_____

_____

_____

_____

PRAYING GOD'S WORD TODAY

God, You are our refuge and strength, a helper who is always found in times of trouble. Therefore we will not be afraid, though the earth trembles and the mountains topple into the depths of the seas, though its waters roar and foam (Ps. 46:1–3). It feels like this sometimes. Stormy and chaotic. At other times, rocky and dry. How I pray that You will pour out Your Spirit from heaven on this place. Then the desert will become an orchard, and the orchard will seem like a forest. Then justice will inhabit the wilderness, and righteousness will dwell in our midst (Isa. 32:15–16). I long for Your transforming power and presence, dear Lord. I need it. I crave it. _____

_____

_____

_____

_____

_____

_____

_____

_____

_____

DAY 65

I'm All Ears

BEFORE YOU BEGIN

Read Revelation 1:12–20

STOP AND CONSIDER

Therefore write what you have seen, what is,
and what will take place after this. (v. 19)

How well do you respond to God when He clearly shows you something from His Word
or in some other form that's definitely Him? _____

_____

_____

Why is obedience to His Word such an important part of our discipleship? What does it
tell us about our true selves? _____

_____

_____

_____

Years ago I learned a good rule of thumb that I've tried to keep before me in study: when plain sense makes common sense, seek no other sense. Through the ages various interpreters have sought to make the churches of Revelation 2–3 symbolic, but what we can know for certain is that they were actual believers and real churches at the time of John's exile. The order of scriptural presentation is actually geographic. All seven cities were located in Asia Minor, and their orders in Scripture suggest a very practical route a messenger might take if he began a journey in Ephesus and traveled on to the other six cities.

We will spend much of our time in Revelation on the messages to the seven churches. The fact that God included the communication in Holy Writ tells us they have something to say to us. In fact, Christ Himself pointed out their relevance to others as He drew all seven letters to a close with a broad invitation, first recorded in Revelation 2:7: "Anyone who has an ear should listen to what the Spirit says to the churches."

Now, feel the side of your head. Do you feel an ear? Try either side, for you only need one: "Anyone who has an ear . . ." If you have one, Jesus would like you to hear what the Spirit says to the churches. I have one, too, so I'm in with you. The reason is obvious. We of His church today have much to learn from the successes, failures, victories, and defeats of the early churches. The generations may be far removed, but our basic nature and the truth of Scripture remain consistent.

Actually, Christ had more in mind than talking to people who had at least one physical ear on the sides of their heads. I certainly had ears throughout my young years, but I'm not sure how well I used them to listen to God. For the most part my ears were important hair accessories. Will I put my hair behind both ears today? One ear? Or shall I let my hair hang over both ears? I was so deep. The messages to the seven churches are for people with a little more depth than that. Christ's broad invitation was more like this: What I've said to them will speak volumes to anyone who really wants to hear and respond. So let's each grab an ear and hear!

PRAYING GOD'S WORD TODAY

O Lord, may I never be like those of whom You said, "Who can I speak to and give such a warning that they will listen? Look, their ear is uncircumcised, so they cannot pay attention. See, the word of the Lord has become contemptible to them—they find no pleasure in it" (Jer. 6:10). Lord, awaken me each morning, awaken my ear to listen like those being instructed, so that I will not be rebellious or turn back from Your Word (Isa. 50:4–5).

DAY 66

Can You Ever Forget
Your First Love?

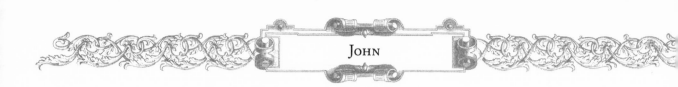
BEFORE YOU BEGIN
Read Revelation 2:1–7

STOP AND CONSIDER

You also possess endurance and have tolerated many things because of My name. . . .

But I have this against you: you have abandoned the love you had at first. (vv. 3–4)

What is it about love—true love for God and the resulting love for others—that outranks and overrides all other character traits and qualities? _____

_____

_____

What causes you to burn low in your supply of love? When and where do you find that it leaks out with the most force and frequency? _____

_____

_____

_____

The letters to the churches in Revelation 2–3 contain several repeated elements that I want you to identify from the very beginning. Although they don't all appear in each of the seven letters, here are the common components:

• *Identification*. Christ identified Himself in a specific way using some element of the first vision in Revelation 1:12–18.

• *Commendation*. While not every letter contains a commendation, all seven include the phrase "I know your . . ." based on His intimate acquaintance with them.

• *Rebuke*. In most cases, He pointed out something that needed correction.

• *Exhortation*. He instructed each church to do something specific.

• *Encouragement*. He always issued an encouragement to overcome. Celebrate the fact that no condition was irreversible!

Using these elements common to each letter to the churches, let's see what Christ had to say to the church at Ephesus.

Identification. Note what Christ pinpoints about Himself to the church in Ephesus: "The One who holds the seven stars in His right hand and who walks among the seven gold lampstands" (2:1). We would be tragically amiss to think Christ is uninvolved and unmoved by the conditions, activities, and inner workings of His present churches. He walks among us. Nothing is more important to Christ in any generation than the health of His church, since it is the vehicle through which He purposes to reach the lost and minister to the hurting.

Commendation. Based on His intimate knowledge of the church of Ephesus, Christ strongly commended them in verses 2 and 3: "I know your works, your labor, and your endurance, and that you cannot tolerate evil. You have tested those who call themselves apostles and are not, and you have found them to be liars. You also possess endurance and have tolerated many things because of My name, and have not grown weary."

Rebuke. "But I have this against you: you have abandoned the love you had at first" (2:4). Remember, the apostle John was most involved in the church at Ephesus. Knowing what we've learned about him, how do you think he responded internally when he heard this particular rebuke concerning his dear ones in Ephesus? He was the pastor who had sought to teach them to love the Lord Christ. Did he feel a sense of failure or reproof?

Exhortation. In verse 5, Christ said, "Remember then how far you have fallen; repent, and do the works you did at first. Otherwise, I will come to you and remove your lampstand from its place—unless you repent." Note a detail about the warning. Christ told the church in Ephesus that if they did not repent and do the things they "did at first," He would come to them and remove their lampstand from its place. The terminology doesn't mean they would lose their place in heaven. We lose our lampstand when we lose a vibrant position of godly influence on earth. In other words, we lose our light in the world.

Hang on to Jesus with every breath and ounce of strength you have. Pray to love Him more than you pray for blessing, health, or ministry.

Encouragement. "I will give the victor the right to eat from the tree of life, which is in the paradise of God" (2:7). The sins of the church at Ephesus weren't hopeless. Nor are ours! Let's repent, though, so we can overcome!

Somehow in my previous studies of this letter, I have overlooked the original meaning of a critical word in the phrase from Christ's rebuke about abandoning or forsaking their first love. I am astonished to find that the original word for "forsaken" is the same word often translated "forgive" in the New Testament. The word *aphiemi* means "to send forth, send away, let go from oneself."[23] The New Testament uses *aphiemi* in many contexts and simply means giving up or letting go of something, such as in the familiar words of Matthew 6:12 (KJV): "Forgive us our debts, as we forgive our debtors."

I could easily sit right here and sob. The thought occurs to me how often we forsake our first love—our indescribably glorious sacred romance—because we refuse to forsake our grudges and grievances. Please allow me to say this with much compassion as one who has been there: We cannot hang on to our sacred romance with Jesus Christ and also our bitterness. We will release one to hang on to the other.

The room unforgiveness is taking up in your life is cheating you of the very thing you were born (again) to experience. Send it forth! Not into oblivion, but into the hands of the faithful and sovereign Judge of the earth. For unless our lampstands are lit with the torch of sacred love, they are nothing but artificial lights. Fluorescent, maybe. But sooner or later, the bulb burns out.

How many times has Christ watched You give up intimacy with Him in order to hang on to unforgiveness? Today, precious one, release the one that is nothing but bondage. Life is too short. What is choking out your love—your first love—for Him? _____

_____

_____

_____

_____

_____

_____

PRAYING GOD'S WORD TODAY

I can hear You say to me, "I remember the loyalty of your youth, your love as a bride—how you followed Me in the wilderness, in a land not sown" (Jer. 2:2). But You also said that love can grow cold (Matt. 24:12). I know it has in me. But if my faith is to flourish, it will only be because my love for You and for others is increasing (2 Thess. 1:3). Surge it in me, Lord, as I freely forgive, refuse to criticize, and grow in grace.

DAY 67

The Sweet Smell
of Real Success

BEFORE YOU BEGIN
Read Revelation 2:8–9

STOP AND CONSIDER

I know your tribulation and poverty, yet you are rich. I know the slander of those
who say they are Jews and are not, but are a synagogue of Satan. (v. 9)

What things do you most desire to be "rich" in? How does a believer in Christ define
abundance and success? _____

_____

_____

Why do so many biblical teachings present us with these kinds of riddles and paradox—
being poor to become rich, giving to receive, dying to discover true life? _____

_____

_____

_____

Christ commented about the slander of those who falsely claimed to be Jews but instead were a synagogue of Satan. This fact may imply that the Jews in Smyrna identified the Christians to the government and greatly heightened the persecution against them.

Imagine God's derision for a people who not only looked the other way but actively enforced poverty and affliction on His children. They had no idea the King of the earth walked through the perfectly paved streets of their fair city checking on those who called themselves by His name.

The people of Smyrna took great pride in the beauty of their city. I found the following quote out of *Biblical Illustrator* quite ironic: "The hills and the sea added to the picturesque quality of the city. The city itself nestled under the hill Pagos, which made an ideal acropolis. This beauty was marred, however, by a drainage problem in the lower city which resulted in the silting up of the harbor and an accumulation of unpleasant odors."[24]

Try as they might to build the most impressive city in Asia, they just couldn't do anything about that putrid smell. Don't think for a moment that their unrelenting persecution of innocent people didn't rise up to the nostrils of God. Interestingly, the name Smyrna means "myrrh."[25] Yet nothing but stench ascended to the heavens from the arrogantly pristine, highly educated, and wealthy of Smyrna. From the hidden slums, however, rose a fragrant incense of great expense. No perfume is more costly and more aromatic to God than the faithfulness of believers who are suffering.

I remember serving on a team with a pastor whose son was soon to die of a malignant brain tumor unless God miraculously intervened. I stood not far from him during praise and worship. This precious father did not deny his immense pain. His tears fell unashamedly, but all the while his worship rose just as unashamedly. I can hardly hold back my own tears as I picture his face. Many of us felt the favor of God over our interdenominational prayer gathering that night. Somehow, I believe in the midst of much praise, a fragrance of greater price and exceeding sweetness ascended to the throne from one grieving servant of God.

Praying God's Word Today

Lord, in ancient days You spoke of Your children in this way: "When I bring you from the peoples and gather you from the countries where you have been scattered, I will accept you as a pleasing aroma. And I will demonstrate My holiness through you in the sight of the nations" (Ezek. 20:41). Oh, may I continue to exude the fragrance of Christ (2 Cor. 2:15) in every setting and situation in which You place me. _____

_____

_____

_____

_____

_____

_____

_____

_____

_____

_____

_____

_____

DAY 68

Killer Exams

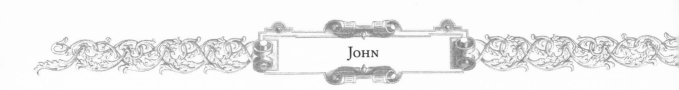
Before You Begin

Read Revelation 2:10–11

Stop and Consider

Look, the Devil is about to throw some of you into prison to test you, and you will have tribulation for 10 days. Be faithful until death, and I will give you the crown of life. (v. 10)

Tests. No one likes them, but the teachers who give them know that they are often the only way to get our attention and to motivate understanding. How are yours doing that? _____

_____

_____

It's easy to say, "Be faithful unto death," but oh, do we even know what that means? How does a person's faith become the kind that even death cannot bully or threaten? _____

_____

_____

_____

Smyrna stands out among the churches as one of two that received no rebuke. As Christ walked beside this lampstand, He found no fault in her.

Impressively, she didn't pass her tests because her exams were easy. To the contrary, no other church is characterized by greater depths of suffering. Christ didn't mince words when He described her afflictions and poverty. Christians were despised and terribly mistreated in Smyrna primarily because no other city in Asia Minor held more allegiance to Rome. The obsessive allegiance of the people of Smyrna became deadly for Christians under the rule of emperors like Nero (AD 54–68) and Domitian (AD 81–96). Anything the emperor reviled, the people of Smyrna reviled. For these two emperors and others that followed, Christians were on the top of the hate list.

How are people like the believers in Smyrna able to be faithful through such terrible suffering? As resistant as we are to absorb it, 1 Peter 1:7 indicates one primary reason: ". . . so that the genuineness of your faith—more valuable than gold, which perishes though refined by fire—may result inc praise, glory, and honor at the revelation of Jesus Christ."

Those who are faithful in the midst of immense suffering somehow allow their fiery trials to purify them rather than destroy them. If we've never suffered like some of the saints we know or have read about, we tend to indict ourselves with failure before our trials ever come. We must remember that God grants us grace and mercy according to our need. No, I do not have the strength or character to be faithful under such heart-shattering conditions. But when my time comes, the Holy Spirit will impart a power and grace I've never experienced. The challenge is whether or not to accept it.

The tragedy is that in our pride and anger we sometimes refuse the grace of God during our times of suffering. The believers in Smyrna did not refuse the grace. They inhaled it like air because they were desperate. As much as the church in Smyrna had suffered, Christ warned them of more to come. He wanted them to be aware, but He did not want them to be afraid. I believe much of the book of Revelation was written to believers for the same purpose.

Mind you, imprisonment and death awaited some of those among the church of Smyrna. We don't know what Christ meant by the time segment of "10 days" in verse 10. Some scholars believe it was literal. Others think it represented ten years. Still others

assume it is a figure of speech for a segment of time known only to God. Whatever the length of trial, Christ called the church of Smyrna to be faithful unto death. His self-identification as the one who died and came to life again reminded them of the absolute assurance of resurrection life. He also promised to reward them with a *stephanos* or victor's crown. They would not be touched by "the second death," a term for the final judgment for all unbelievers.

> Those who are faithful in the midst of immense suffering somehow allow their fiery trials to purify them rather than destroy them.

Sometimes Jesus defines "overcoming" not as living well but dying well. In other words, dying with faith and spiritual dignity. Beloved, dying is the one thing each of us is going to do unless we're the chosen generation to "meet the Lord in the air" without tasting death (1 Thess. 4:17).

At least one of the saints in Smyrna to which Christ addressed His letter left us a profound and wonderful example of an overcoming death. His name was Polycarp. He studied directly under the apostle John's tutelage and was alive at the time the Revelation was penned. He became the bishop of the church in Smyrna and served the generation that followed John's heavenly departure. *Foxe's Book of Martyrs* shares the following account of Polycarp's trial and martyrdom.

He was, however, carried before the proconsul, condemned. . . . The proconsul then urged him, saying, 'Swear, and I will release thee;—reproach Christ.' Polycarp answered, 'Eighty and six years have I served Him, and He has done me no wrong. How then can I blaspheme my King who has saved me?' At the stake to which he was only tied, not nailed as usual, as he assured them he should stand immovable, the flames, on their kindling the fagots, encircled his body, like an arch, without touching him; and the executioner, on seeing this, was ordered to pierce him with a sword, when so great a quantity of blood flowed out as extinguished the fire.[26]

He had overcome. As long as those moments must have been, nothing could have prepared Polycarp for the sight he beheld when death gave way to life and faith gave way to sight. The only Jesus he had ever seen was in the face and heart of John the Beloved. But that day the old bishop of Smyrna saw the One he loved and had served for eighty and six years. Face to face. With a victor's crown in His hand.

When I get to heaven and meet him, I'm going to try to remember to ask Polycarp if he thought his suffering was worth it. Oh, I already know the answer . . . but I want to see his expression.

How do I ask you a question about suffering that hasn't already been asked a million times before? What about this: Where would any of us be today had it not been for seasons of suffering? If everything always went our way, what kind of people would we probably be?

_____

_____

_____

_____

PRAYING GOD'S WORD TODAY

Father, how desperately we, Your children, need the renewing of our mind, so that we may discern Your good, pleasing, and perfect will (Rom. 12:2). In our human ways of thinking, overcoming a life-threatening situation always means staying alive! But Your Word teaches that the death of Your faithful ones is valuable in Your sight (Ps. 116:15), and that the day of one's death is better than the day of one's birth (Eccles. 7:1). How hard to grasp what these mean, and yet I pray for understanding—that I may live in the present-day reality of resurrection life!

DAY 69

Fakes among
the Faithful

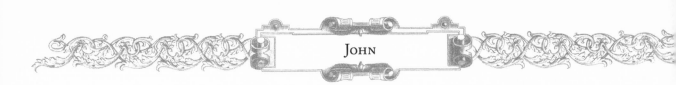
Before You Begin
Read Revelation 2:12–13

Stop and Consider
The One who has the sharp, two-edged sword says:
I know where you live—where Satan's throne is! (vv. 12–13)

Seeing Christ with a "two-edged sword" means no one gets counted among His church simply by showing up. What lure does the church have for those who don't really want Christ as Lord? _____

_____

_____

What do you think life in the vicinity of "Satan's throne" would have been like? Where do you think he sits most comfortably today? _____

_____

_____

_____

We can only imagine what kind and level of warfare the young church in Pergamum experienced. Christ referred to the city as the place "where Satan's throne is." Since Satan is not omnipresent, this claim is hair-raising. We can't be certain what Christ meant, but historical evidence from the first century tells us Pergamum was the uncontested center of pagan worship in Asia Minor.

Keep in mind that Satan's primary goal is to keep people blinded to the truth while providing them with something that momentarily seems to assuage their spiritual hunger. Pergamum delivered. Christ spoke about the church in Pergamum remaining true to His name. Goodness knows, inhabitants had plenty of names to choose from. Within its walls were temples to Dionysus, Athena, Asclepius, and Demeter; three temples to the emperor cult; and a huge altar to Zeus.

Although the philosophy of the city seemed to be "pick a god, any god," two primary religions exceeded all others in Pergamum: the worship of Dionysus, considered god of the royal kings (symbolized by the bull), and the worship of Asclepius, called "the savior god of healing" (symbolized by the snake). Does that second title make your skin crawl like it does mine? I know the Savior God of Healing, and I assure you it isn't the snake. God heals in many ways, but He alone is Jehovah Rapha. I'm reminded of God's words in Hosea 11:3. The prophet said of Israel, "They never knew that I healed them." All healing is meant to reveal the Healer, so Satan will do anything he can to block the connection.

The first psalm I memorized was Psalm 103. I still love it. It urges us to praise the Lord and not to forget His benefits. This is especially important because, given the opportunity, Satan gladly supplies a counterfeit "savior" who claims to provide a dandy benefit package. Any world religion or brand of humanism will do.

But man was created to seek God's benefits. That's why Satan works most effectively if he is able to offer alternatives. For instance, he's sly to suggest other ways for people to unload their guilt. One workable way is to convince them they haven't sinned. He has all sorts of means of providing counterfeit "redemption." Don't fall for them—any of them!

Praying God's Word Today

Lord Jesus, You warned us that false messiahs and false prophets would arise and perform great signs and wonders to lead astray, if possible, even the elect. "Take note," You said, "I have told you in advance" (Matt. 24:24–25). Keep me sensitive, Lord, to the dangers that come disguised as truth, choosing instead to dwell in Your Word. The entirety of Your word is truth, and all Your righteous judgments endure forever (Ps. 119:160). _____

DAY 70

Satan, Seduction, and a White Stone

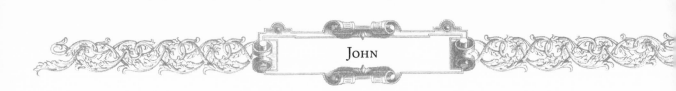

Before You Begin

Read Revelation 2:14–17

Stop and Consider

I will also give him a white stone, and on the stone a new name
is inscribed that no one knows except the one who receives it. (v. 17)

Satan can seduce, and the world can entice, but real blessing only awaits the faithful. What
keeps you encouraged when you're tempted to quit or at least to compromise? _____

_____

_____

We don't know exactly what this "new name" is talking about, but if you could think of
some nouns or adjectives you'd like to be known by forever, what would they be? _____

_____

_____

_____

Not long ago I received a letter from a loved one with whom I shared my testimony about the transforming power of God's Word. He, a practicing Buddhist, wrote me his own testimony about how life had improved since he changed his "karma." My heart broke over the inevitable disillusionment of self-worship. At some point surely a self-worshiper looks in the mirror and says, "If I am as good as God gets, life really stinks." And yet counterfeits continue to be sold and manufactured on every corner.

Christ, for example, rebuked an undesignated number in Pergamum for holding to the teachings of Balaam and the Nicolaitans. The fact that He commanded the repentance of the whole church means the number had to be significant. Although God esteems repentance of the faithful on behalf of the unfaithful, He doesn't require it from people who haven't sinned. Look back at His commendation to the church of Ephesus in Revelation 2:2. I suspect the church in Pergamum may have tolerated "wicked men" and false apostles more than the church of Ephesus.

We can't dogmatically identify the teaching of the Nicolaitans, but they are closely associated with the teachings of Balaam. The account of Balaam and Balak is found in Numbers 22–24. In a nutshell, Balak, the king of Moab, greatly feared the Israelites as they settled in the promised land. He hired Balaam the soothsayer to curse Israel, but Balaam blessed them instead. He did, however, instruct Balak how to defeat the Israelites. He told Balak to seduce them into idolatry through the harlotry of the Moabite women. Based on all I've read, I believe the basic concept of Balaam's teachings is this: If you can't curse them, try to seduce them!

The whole idea makes my blood boil. You see, Satan is waging war on our generation with Balaam's weapon (see 1 Tim. 4:1). Satan can't curse us because we are blessed (Eph. 1:3)—children of God, covered by the blood of the Lamb. If the devil can't curse us, then how can he defeat us? He can try to seduce us! How does seduction differ from temptation? All seduction is temptation, but not all temptation is seduction. Many temptations are just plain obvious and outright. The aim of seduction, on the other hand, is to catch the prey off guard. That's why Satan's best henchmen (or women) are often insiders rather than outsiders. Some in the church of Pergamum were being enticed into sin by others among them, and Christ expected the church to jump to action.

Many temptations are just plain obvious and outright. The aim of seduction, on the other hand, is to catch the prey off guard.

Whether or not the seducers were truly saved is unclear. If the seducers were indeed true believers, they needed to be confronted properly and restored when repentant. Some may wonder how believers could be used by Satan to seduce. Beloved, seduced people seduce people. And if the devil's scheme is not exposed and the chain is not broken, it perpetuates. We must develop discernment and guard our hearts jealously without becoming fearful and suspicious. Authentic godliness rather than religiousness is our best defense against seduction.

Christ's letter to the church in Pergamum must have hit hard, but the tenderness and encouragement of the conclusion spared their hearts.

Christ promised two things to those who overcame: hidden manna and a white stone. The hidden manna contrasts beautifully with the food sacrificed to idols. Jesus Christ was the Bread of Life sacrificed on the altar before the one true God. Now His Spirit falls like manna from heaven to all who hunger. Jewish tradition holds that the ark with the pot of manna in it was hidden by order of King Josiah and will be revealed once again during the earthly reign of the Messiah.

The most probable meaning of the white stone in verse 17 is remarkable. In an ancient courtroom, jurors voting to condemn the accused would cast their vote by tossing a black stone or pebble. In contrast, jurors voting to acquit the condemned would cast their vote by tossing a white stone or pebble. Scripture actually records this ancient practice, but our English translations don't portray it. In the course of sharing his testimony, Paul said he "cast my vote against" the Christians (Acts 26:10). The original wording is *katenegka psephon*. The Greek word *katenegka* means "to deposit or cast." The Greek word *psephon* means "pebble or stone," and is only used in Acts 26:10 and Revelation 2:17.[27] Paul formerly deposited or cast his pebble to vote against the saints.

If we're on target, the terminology Christ used was perfectly fitting for Pergamum, which was the legal center of the district. How I praise God that the Judge of all the earth pitches a white stone to acquit us—not because we're innocent but because Someone has already served our sentence. And the new name on the stone? It could be Christ's, but I also think we each have an overcoming name that's unique and individual to us, not unlike Abram had Abraham, Simon had Peter, and Saul had Paul.

I'll be honest with you. I'll be glad to leave Pergamum and its insider seducers. But the manna and the stone? Those were worth the trip. See you tomorrow in Thyatira!

Where do you find yourself most commonly seduced? What lies do you deal with and fend off on a fairly daily basis?

_____

_____

_____

_____

_____

_____

Praying God's Word Today

Father, You have said that to those who hold firmly to Your covenant, You would give them—in Your house and within Your walls—a memorial and a name better than sons and daughters, an everlasting name that will never be cut off (Isa. 56:4–5). I sit here in stunned awe at such graciousness, poured out on one like me. A new name. I can't think of a better gift You could give me. Thank You for always being a God of newness.

DAY 71

Tale of Two Women

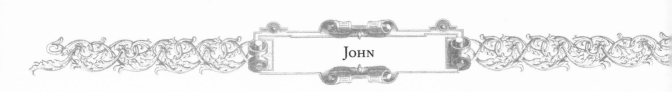

BEFORE YOU BEGIN

Read Revelation 2:18–29

STOP AND CONSIDER

You tolerate the woman Jezebel, who calls herself a prophetess, and teaches and deceives My slaves to commit sexual immorality and to eat meat sacrificed to idols. (v. 20)

There's a good reason why you don't see many (dare I say "any") new baby girls named Jezebel in the maternity wing. What does "Jezebel" represent in your mind? _____

_____

_____

In a culture so saturated as ours with sexually charged images and innuendo, what can you do personally to reclaim the purity of God's ideal and to have a positive impact for good?

_____

_____

_____

Scripture associates Thyatira with two different women: Lydia and Jezebel. Acts 16:13–15 tells about Lydia, the businesswoman who became the first named convert in Europe. Lydia was from Thyatira. I love the words of verse 14 (NIV): "The Lord opened her heart to respond to Paul's message." Then her entire household followed Christ.

Then there's Jezebel. Some scholars interpret Jezebel as a reference to a false doctrine, a type of demonic spirit, or a behavioral concept. Others believe she was a flesh-and-blood woman who played havoc in the church at Thyatira. I am strongly inclined to agree with the latter, but I am also thoroughly convinced she is representative of a kind of woman none of us want to be.

The Revelation 2 Jezebel was a very powerful woman in Thyatira. Likely up to her elbows in secret guilds and society climbs, she did everything she could to infiltrate the church with them. Lydia was also a powerful woman in Thyatira. Together they provide a lesson on abuse versus wise use of authority. Let's perform a character sketch of Jezebel and invite Lydia to hold up a lamp of contrast in her counterpart's insidious darkness.

1. *Jezebel assumed places of authority God did not assign her* (v. 20). Before you jump to the conclusion that her infraction was assuming a role that could belong only to men, note that the New Testament undeniably records the viability of a woman having the God-given gift of prophecy, or what we might generalize as "speaking forth" (Luke 2:36–37; Acts 2:17–18; Acts 21:8–9). Jezebel had no such God-given gift. She wasn't called. She was controlling! She wasn't wisely authoritative. She was bossy! Oh, that none of us—male or female—would confuse the two!

Certainly God calls women into places of leadership, but in the spirit of 1 Corinthians 11:5, I believe our heads must be covered by higher authority. I cannot express how strongly I feel about this issue. As women, we enjoy a wonderful umbrella of protection. The biblical, proverbial buck stops with the men of our households and churches. If God calls a woman to assume a leadership role, I believe with all my heart she is only safe and operating in God's authentic anointing under that umbrella!

Given my past and my lack of credentials, I will never understand the sovereignty of God to appoint *me* to an area of leadership. At the same time, I know what He has called me to do for this season, and I'd be in direct disobedience to God if I let someone's disapproval dissuade me. I cannot describe, however, the terror that shoots through me over finding myself here. How anyone can have an intimate relationship with God and be arrogant and fearless in a position of authority is beyond me.

James 3:1 warns, "Not many should become teachers, my brothers, knowing that we will receive a stricter judgment." Why would anyone ask for "stricter judgment"? Jezebel was asking for it whether she knew it or not. Please don't miss that Jezebel's most serious infraction was not her sin but her unwillingness to repent! Lydia stands in stark contrast to Jezebel as a woman of success. She was a worshiper of God—not of herself or position. She opened her heart to Paul's message rather than pull rank on him. Both professionally and spiritually, the tone of Scripture suggests she was a servant leader.

> Many women have strong gifts and rise to the top in various professions. But if not submitted to the true liberation of Christ's authority, we can be terrifying.

2. *Jezebel abused her feminine gift of influence* (v. 20). She misled and deceived. I am convinced that women have a unique God-given gift of influence. I am married to a very strong man. He no doubt wears the cowboy boots in our family. But, if I used my feminine wiles just right (or just wrong), I fear I could talk him into almost anything. I have to be very careful because he loves me and wants to please me. You see, in some ways I am his weakness. Do you understand what I mean?

Many accounts in Scripture attest to the power of a woman's influence. Eve and Sarai represent some biblical blights but, thankfully, we can find many more scriptural examples of positive womanly influence than negative. Lydia is certainly one of them. She influenced her whole household to follow Christ.

3. *Jezebel misused her sexuality* (v. 21). Sisters, I'm not sure our culture has taught us to use anything more powerfully than our sexuality. Don't think for a moment that seducing someone into fornication is the only way a woman can use her sexuality to manipulate. We can be completely clothed and in broad, public daylight and still misuse our sexuality.

I might have a sister in Christ who is horrified right this minute by our discussion of this tawdry topic. True, she may never have dreamed of using her sexuality seductively or manipulatively. Then again, this same woman may wield it like a massive weapon in her marriage.

Sexuality was given by God as a gift. Not a tool. Just because we're married doesn't mean we don't horrifically misuse our sexuality to get what we want. Routine withholding is just one example. God created us to be women complete with all our gifts, contributions, and influences. But let's be women well.

What do you love most about being a woman? What aspects are the most troublesome?

_____

_____

_____

_____

_____

_____

_____

PRAYING GOD'S WORD TODAY

Lord, I receive Your Word that says older women are to be reverent in behavior, not slanderers, not addicted to much wine. We are to teach what is good, so that we may encourage the young women to love their husbands and children, to be sensible, pure, good homemakers, and submissive to their husbands, so that God's message will not be slandered. (Titus 2:3–5). I want to be a woman after Your own heart.

DAY 72

One Foot in the Grave

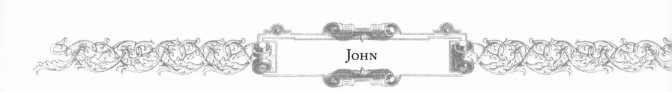
Before You Begin

Read Revelation 3:1–6

Stop and Consider

Be alert and strengthen what remains, which is about to die,

for I have not found your works complete before My God. (v. 2)

Has anything happened to take the wind out of your sails? To cause you to drop your arms and cease defending yourself against the enemy? To leave works incomplete? _____

_____

_____

What work do you believe is still undone in your life, even though fatigue and lethargy sometimes make you not feel like trying anymore? _____

_____

_____

_____

If we studied the seven churches of Asia Minor and seven hundred more in our cities today, we would quickly discover a disturbing fact. The personalities and moral attitudes of any given city permeate its churches unless the church works to deliberately overcome. For instance, churches in wealthy areas with upper-crust attitudes will have to overcome misguided superiority to keep from portraying the same things. Why? Because the people who comprise churches are also products of their societies. Likewise, churches in cities of deeply ingrained prejudice will carry the same banner unless they deliberately risk being different. A church can be refreshingly dissimilar to its surrounding society only through deliberately renewing their minds.

We might accurately say that the city surrounding the church of Sardis had nearly killed it. Christ had little to say in favor of this ancient church. In fact, I can think of few indictments more serious to a group of believers than these three words: "You are dead" (Rev. 3:1). I believe dead churches are one of the most confounding mysteries to the hosts of heaven. The ministering spirits that invisibly flood the atmosphere must look on the church then back on the radiance of Jesus Christ and wonder how anything that carries His name can be dead. Above all things, Christ is life!

What invaded the church of Sardis with such deadness? The history of this ancient city suggests three permeating contributors:

1. *The people of Sardis were fixated on death rather than life.* Perhaps you'll be as interested as I was to learn that Sardis was best known for a necropolis called the "cemetery of the thousand hills" about seven miles from town. Can you imagine a city known for its cemeteries? But where burial mounds become idols, thoughts of death overtake thoughts of life. I once received a letter from a sister in Christ who was alarmed that I mentioned visiting the graveside of a friend. She was not unkind. She was simply surprised that anyone who believed so strongly in heaven would esteem meaningless remains by visiting a grave. Though I didn't agree with her philosophy, if I were more focused on my believing friend's death than her life, my sister would have a point.

But we don't have to idolize burial mounds like the Sardians to focus on death more than life. Worship in its simplest essence is attentiveness. One way we can focus on death more than life is to possess a life-inhibiting fear of it. I have known people who were so scared of death they could hardly live. You might say they were worshiping burial mounds much like the Sardians—whether or not they realized it. A chronic fear of death can inhibit a believer's entire life and ministry.

> I have known people who were so scared of death they could hardly live. A chronic fear of death can inhibit our lives.

2. *The people of Sardis relied on their past achievements*. Sardis was like a leading lady in a Greek tragedy who waltzed around town in riches turned to rags thinking everyone still saw her as she was thirty years ago. In essence, Christ wrote the church of Sardis to hand this self-deceived woman a mirror—just like He's handed one to me a time or ten. Christ does not hand someone a mirror to destroy, however. He hands her the mirror to wake her up!

I was invited a few years ago to attend some special homecoming festivities at my college alma mater. I greatly enjoyed renewing friendships and acquaintances. But I was mystified and somewhat amused as I watched other people "time warp," holding a death grip on the past. If time warping weren't so pitiful, it would be hilarious. Sardis was warped by time. She lived off her past fame, and the results were tragic. Unfortunately, the church within its walls had followed suit.

3. *The people of Sardis likely interpreted rejection as a deathblow*. Though the city of Sardis housed an incomplete temple of Artemis, they lost their bid to build a temple to Caesar in AD 26. Smyrna won the bid instead. Though the church of Sardis had nothing but disdain for pagan practices and temples, my hypothesis is that the people of the church unknowingly wore the same cloak of dejected identity as their surroundings. After all, they too were pagans until the gospel reached their gates—most likely under the preaching of the

apostle Paul. I'd like to further hypothesize that the people of Sardis knew they needed a fresh shot of life and vitality when they bid Rome for the new temple. When they were rejected in favor of a rival city, I wonder if they took on an attitude all too common after rejection: Who cares anymore? Unless good reason exists to respond otherwise, rejection can cause people to lose heart faster than almost anything else.

Perhaps the following commentary best sums up the deadness of Sardis at the time of John's vision: "Sardis was a city of peace. Not the peace won through battle, but the peace of a man whose dreams are dead and whose mind is asleep. The peace of lethargy and evasion."[28] I find that statement stunning not because it speaks so perfectly to an ancient city's decay but because it speaks to many of us today.

Dead churches, you know, are made up of lifeless Christians. In what way do you see this perhaps taking place in your own congregation? What can you and others do about it?

_____

_____

_____

_____

_____

_____

PRAYING GOD'S WORD TODAY

Lord, the only death I want to carry around in my body is the death of Jesus, so that the life of Jesus may also be revealed in me (2 Cor. 4:10). For the mind-set of the flesh is death, but the mind-set of the Spirit is life and peace (Rom. 8:6). Infuse me, Lord with Your never-ending life.

DAY 73

Little Matters

BEFORE YOU BEGIN

Read Revelation 3:7–8

STOP AND CONSIDER

Because you have limited strength, have kept My word, and have not denied My name,

look, I have placed before you an open door that no one is able to close. (v. 8)

You may feel like you possess "limited" strength, "limited" resources, "limited" potential. But are you letting your "limits" define your purpose in life? How? _____

_____

_____

Christ honored this church's faithfulness with blessing, despite its obvious shortages of supply. How have you seen this proven in your life or in situations you're familiar with?

_____

_____

_____

Scholars almost unanimously agree that the reference in Revelation 2:8 to the "little" or "limited" strength of the church in Philadelphia was not to spiritual strength, or Christ would not have placed the characteristic in context with such commendation. Christ never commends spiritual weakness. Rather, He views weakness as an opportunity to discover a divine strength beyond our imagination (2 Cor. 12:9–10). Bible commentators believe this referred to their diminutive size and small visible impact, to the fact that lower, less influential classes comprised the church in this city.

In our numbers-oriented society, we can hardly overestimate when we see ourselves as ineffective. I believe outright opposition can often be easier to bear than the thought of futility or incompetence. And don't think for a moment the enemy won't do everything he can to convince you that your efforts in Christ's name are in vain. Nothing is more destructive than feelings of uselessness and worthlessness. That's precisely why the enemy seeks every avenue to fuel and perpetuate them.

Beloved, each of us has a God-given need to matter. You are not self-centered and vain because you have that need; you are human. Sure, the things you and I do with this need can become extremely vain and self-centered, but the need itself is sacred. Fragrant flowers don't need someone to smell them to keep blooming. Lions don't kill their prey for significance—they're simply hungry. Only man yearns to matter.

God acknowledged this need immediately following our creation and before our fall into sin. Notice how He granted purpose to humans in each of these scriptural examples.

- He gave the assignment to be fruitful, fill the earth, and have dominion (Gen. 1:28).
- He gave Adam the charge to care for the garden (Gen. 2:15).
- He commissioned Adam to name the animals (Gen. 2:19).

God could have created the beasts of the field naturally subservient to humans. Instead, He acknowledged our God-given need to matter by telling us to rule over them and subdue them. Furthermore, God could have made the garden of Eden self-maintaining. Instead, He appointed Adam to work it and take care of it. God could have created the animals with names, but He knew Adam could use the challenge and the satisfaction that naming them would bring. In the same way, Eve received a purpose that granted significance. No one else was a suitable helper to Adam.

> God not only allows long seasons of seedtime but also sometimes appoints them to enhance the quality of eventual harvest.

The Father desires for each of our lives to matter—to bring forth much fruit. The small, seemingly insignificant band of believers in Philadelphia may have been blind to the fruit of their own efforts, but Christ found them beyond rebuke. I think the key word in His commendation is the description He used in verse 10 (NIV) for how they endured: "patiently." So often we are tempted to give up before the harvest comes.

Ecclesiastes 3:1 tells us, "There is an occasion for everything, and a time for every activity under heaven." God promised, "As long as the earth endures, seedtime and harvest, cold and heat, summer and winter, and day and night will not cease" (Gen. 8:22). Though far less predictable than these natural seasons, we experience seasons spiritually as well. The church in Philadelphia had been in the seedtime season without a large harvest probably longer than they wished—yet they continued to endure patiently.

Do you happen to be frustrated by what appears to be a small return on much effort in a ministry opportunity? Keep in mind that God not only allows long seasons of seedtime but also sometimes *appoints* them to enhance the quality of eventual harvest. At times He actively tests our faithfulness in smaller things to see if we can handle bigger things. I hesitate to make this point, because "big" is not the goal; Christ revealed is the goal. However, if a high-volume ministry is one way God chooses to reveal His Son, those to whom He temporarily appoints them by His grace (1 Pet. 4:10) could undoubtedly describe countless appointments to small and frustrating "opportunities" along the way. In retrospect, most now recognize these as crucial tests.

I can remember pouring my heart into preparing several discipleship courses when only two or three people showed up. I sensed God asking me, "What are you going to do now? Cancel the class? Or give them no less than you would give if twenty-five people were here, eager to finish out the semester?" I am certain those were not only precious opportunities; they were tests. I also believe He tested me to see whether I would esteem the opportunity to teach Mother's Day Out or four-year-olds in Sunday school. Both extended the profound opportunity to mark young lives for eternity, yet some would be foolish enough to deem them unimportant.

Thankfully, we obviously don't have to be a genius or particularly gifted to pass God's tests because I certainly would have failed. God is primarily looking for faithfulness to fulfill whatever duty He has placed before us. He formed us to seek lives of purpose and, for those of us who follow His lead, to find them ultimately in Him alone.

Perhaps you find it revolutionary to hear that our desire to matter comes from God Himself. If you were free from feeling apologetic about this, how would it change your perspective on things and your life's direction? _____

_____

_____

_____

_____

PRAYING GOD'S WORD TODAY

I call to You today, God Most High, the One who fulfills Your purpose for me (Ps. 57:2), knowing that when Your people take delight in You, Lord, You do indeed give us our heart's desires (Ps. 37:4). Lord, Your love is eternal. Do not abandon the work of Your hands (Ps. 138:8). Continue in me all You have planned, and thank You for making the process of living it a sacred blessing all its own. _____

DAY 74

Eat Those Words

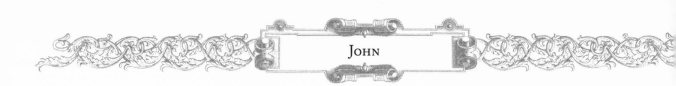
BEFORE YOU BEGIN

Read Revelation 3:9–13

STOP AND CONSIDER

I will make them come and bow down at your feet,

and they will know that I have loved you. (v. 9)

What are some of the insulting, derogatory things that people say about Christian faith? How have you felt it, not just in general terms but personally—directed right at you? _____

_____

_____

Perhaps nothing would ever convince these individuals that Jesus is love. But what could they see in you that might make them wonder? _____

_____

_____

_____

One of the meanest tricks Satan ever plays on us is to try convincing us God doesn't love us and that we're exerting all this energy and exercising all this faith for nothing: "Look at all you've done, and He doesn't even care! It's all a big joke!" Detect the smell of devil breath in a statement like that?

Drawn from this passage in Revelation 3, we discover that Satan used the Jews in Philadelphia to demoralize this small church, just as he uses countless puppets in our own lives and times to demoralize us. But Christ promised the church in this city that one day the very people who sneered at them would acknowledge something they would never have confessed on their own. In the end, they would be forced to admit just how much He loves them.

Beloved, you and I are not to be motivated by spite. At the same time, Jesus wants you to know that one day everyone will know how much He loves you. You have been unashamed of Him, and He most assuredly will prove unashamed of you.

What a show of His love, then, that Christ promised to make these overcomers pillars in the temple of God (v. 12). Philadelphia was a city under constant threat of earthquakes. The threat was especially vivid after a devastating earthquake in AD 17. Decades later, some historians say the church had already rebuilt their small sanctuary several times because of tremors. Often the only things left standing in a city lying in ruins are the pillars.

Hebrews 12:26–27 says God will shake both the heavens and the earth so that only that which cannot be shaken will remain. "Therefore, since we are receiving a kingdom that cannot be shaken, let us hold on to grace. By it, we may serve God acceptably, with reverence and awe; for our God is a consuming fire" (Heb. 12:28–29).

Christ's promise to the overcomers was that they would be kept from the hour of trial coming upon the whole world, and they would stand like pillars in a kingdom that can never be shaken. Why? Because they were loved and, contrary to popular opinion, they chose to believe it. You, too, are loved, dear one. Let no one take your crown by convincing you otherwise.

PRAYING GOD'S WORD TODAY

Not to us, Lord, not to us, but to Your name give glory because of Your faithful love, because of Your truth (Ps. 115:1). You remember us in our humiliation and will rescue us from our foes. Your love indeed is eternal (Ps. 136:23–24).

DAY 75

Hot and Cold

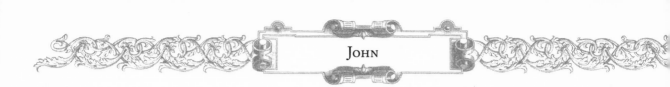
BEFORE YOU BEGIN

Read Revelation 3:14–16

STOP AND CONSIDER

I know your works, that you are neither cold nor hot. I wish that you were cold or hot. So, because you are lukewarm . . . I am going to vomit you out of My mouth. (vv. 15–16)

What are some of the characteristics of "lukewarm" Christianity? _____

_____

_____

Why are these attitudes and expressions so distasteful and unsatisfying? _____

_____

_____

_____

_____

_____

We can safely conclude that Christ would not prefer anyone to be spiritually "cold" toward Him rather than lukewarm, which is the way some have interpreted this passage. I believe Christ meant, "For crying out loud, be of one use or the other!" We have much to learn about this distinct city that will shed light on Christ's rebuke and exhortation.

Laodicea lay directly between two other cities, seven miles southeast of Hierapolis and less than ten miles north of Colossae. Hierapolis was famous for therapeutic hot springs. Colossae was known for sparkling cold waters, but ruins reveal a sophisticated six-mile-long aqueduct that drew water from other sources for Laodicea.

In 1961–63 a team of French archaeologists excavated a structure called a *nymphaeum* located practically in the center of the city. The square water basin had stone columns on two sides and two semicircular fountains attached to it.[29] The ornate fountains very likely stood as beautiful centerpieces in the city square. Characteristic of Laodicea, their beauty vastly exceeded their usefulness. You see, by the time the water was piped to the city from miles away, it was neither cold nor hot. You might easily imagine someone cupping her hands under the enticing waters to take a refreshing sip only to spit it out in disgust. Sound familiar? Hot water has therapeutic value, and nothing is like the refreshment of cold water, but lukewarm? If only I knew the Greek word for "yuck!"

Christ's vehement frustration with the church of Laodicea was that she'd be of some use! The last thing I want to tout is a works-centered faith, but we have been called to faith-centered works. Christ intends for us to be useful! Churches are meant to be viable, active forces in their communities.

We talked earlier about how each person's innate need to matter requires us to discover how our gifts and contributions can be useful. In the spirit of Christ's exhortation to Laodicea, anyone can offer a cold glass of water to the thirsty or a hot cup of tea to the hurting. Or how about a frozen casserole? Or a warm pound cake? At times of my life, nothing has ministered to me more than those two things! Christ exhorts His bride, "Be of use to my world!" At times therapeutic. At other times refreshing. Each of us can be hot *and* cold.

PRAYING GOD'S WORD TODAY

Father, Your Word says that "good news from a distant land is like cold water to a parched throat" (Prov. 25:25), and that anyone who gives a cup of cold water to a brother or sister will never lose his reward (Matt. 10:42). Yet Jeremiah said that Your Word within him was like a fire burning in his heart, unable to be held in, desperately needing to be shared with others (Jer. 20:9). May I grasp the value of these two dimensions of usefulness— serving and proclaiming, helping and inspiring. May I be both hot and cold.

DAY 76

What Do You Need?

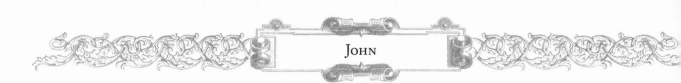

BEFORE YOU BEGIN

Read Revelation 3:17–22

STOP AND CONSIDER

You say, "I'm rich; I have become wealthy, and need nothing,"
and you don't know that you are wretched, pitiful, poor, blind, and naked. (v. 17)

Being very honest, has there been a time when, deep down inside, you thought you "needed nothing," that you could manage just fine on your own? What brought this about? _____

_____

_____

How did the Lord use life and circumstances to correct your faulty vision? What would have happened to you if He hadn't? _____

_____

_____

_____

The Laodiceans did what many people in our culture do today. They filled their gaping need to matter with possessions, then gauged their usefulness by their wealth. Praise God, neither then nor now can wealth state worth.

Save your breath trying to convince Laodicea, however. When Christ drafted His letter to John, Laodicea was the capital of financial wizardry in Asia Minor, a marvel of prosperity. She described herself as rich and in need of nothing (Rev. 3:17).

I discovered some interesting pieces of information that help explain the audacity and laxity of the Laodicean church. In AD 26 the city placed a bid to the Roman senate to build a temple to the Emperor Tiberius. They were denied on the basis of inadequate resources. But their wealth so vastly increased over the next several decades that by AD 60 after the devastation of an earthquake, they didn't accept aid from Nero. They had plentiful resources to rebuild themselves. (Do you hear the hints of independence?) In a nutshell, they thanked Rome but assured them they didn't need a thing.

Money. The Laodiceans had it. They were in the lap of luxury and didn't think they had a care in the world. Little did they know, however, that Christ was walking among their lampstands.

The last portion of Psalm 62:10 (NIV) speaks a good word to the Laodiceans—as well as to us. "Though your riches increase, do not set your heart on them." I live in a city that never expected to be known for the collapse of one of the biggest financial empires in America. We learned the sobering lesson that billions of dollars can be lost as instantly as hundreds. We cannot set our hearts securely on riches no matter how vast.

In Matthew 13:22, Christ addressed another wealth-related issue readily recognizable in Laodicea. He told of the person who received the Word but then allowed "the worries of this age and the seduction of wealth" to choke the fruitfulness out of it. Beloved, wealth by itself is not the issue. We serve a God of infinite wealth who can distribute the riches of the world any way He sees fit. Our troubled world certainly needs resources in the hands of wise people. The problem is the "seduction" or "deceitfulness" of wealth.

Two of my precious friends have not been deceived by wealth. Frankly, I never knew they were wealthy at all until someone told me. I've served in the same church with them for several decades and have never met less pretentious, more generous people. They are constantly involved in inner-city and foreign missions. I'm convinced their only attitude toward their resources is that of stewards over a trust. While others in their position might have locked themselves behind gates and pretended much of the world wasn't starving to death, they threw themselves right in the middle of it.

Christ has invested everything on earth in His church. He fills her, frees her, purifies her, and restores her, but He never takes His eyes off her.

The Laodicean church could have used my friends! This wealthy church somehow didn't grasp the principle in Luke 12:48 (KJV): "Unto whomsoever much is given, of him shall be much required." Their worth was so ingrained in their wealth that they honestly saw themselves as utterly independent. We "need nothing." Famous last words.

The older I get and the more my eyes open to the facts of life and ministry, the more my list of needs exceeds my list of wants. For instance, I need to have an active, effervescent daily relationship with Jesus Christ or I'm sunk. I need my husband's blessing. I need my coworkers. I need my church family. I need a friend I can trust. These are just a few necessities of life to me right now.

You see, one reason we readily give is because we, too, need. Taking stock of both our contributions and our needs helps guard us against self-deception. The Laodiceans had needs, too. They just didn't recognize them. But—praise be to God—their self-deceived indifference had not deemed them castaways. Christ had a stunning response and remedy to the Laodicean deception (verse 18).

His first prescription was "gold refined in the fire." Peter gives us a clear idea of what Christ meant. Peter wrote of "your faith—more valuable than gold" (1 Pet. 1:6–7).

Christ's second prescription to Loadicea was "white clothes" to wear. The black wool fabric for which Laodicea was famous was the fashion rage all over that part of the world. He suggested they trade their fashions for purity. Ouch.

Jesus' final prescription was "ointment to spread on your eyes." Not only was Laodicea a marketing and financial capital, it also housed a well-known medical center. Ever the marketers, they were best known for Phrygian powder that was used to make salve for eye conditions. All the while, they were blind as bats and poor as beggars. I've been both.

One thing I've learned about God is that He is faithful in every way. He is faithful to forgive, redeem, bless, and provide. He is also faithful to chastise when His child won't readily turn from sin. Yes, the Laodiceans had a prescription, but Christ had no intention of letting them wait a month of Sundays to get it filled without consequences.

This concludes our seven-city tour through the ancient Near East. What have been some of the high spots of the trip for you? If someone were to ask you what you learned most from visiting these seven churches, what would you tell them? _____

_____

_____

_____

_____

_____

PRAYING GOD'S WORD TODAY

Lord Jesus, You are the head of the body, the church. You are the beginning, the firstborn from the dead, so that You might come to have first place in everything (Col. 1:18). Have first place in my church. Have first place in my life. Have first place in all Your people, that we may be exactly who You desire us to be on the earth, looking forward to the day when we will be at home with You forever.

DAY 77

Beside the Crystal Sea

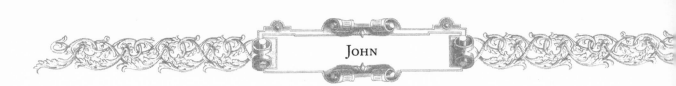
BEFORE YOU BEGIN

Read Revelation 4:1–6a

STOP AND CONSIDER

Also before the throne was something like a sea of glass, similar to crystal. (v. 6a)

Hard to imagine this kind of beauty, isn't it? How do the things that sparkle and shine in your own life look after you've witnessed scenes like these in your mind's eye? _____

_____

_____

The word for this is "glory"—His awesomeness, His brilliance, His splendor. What can you do to keep this high, lofty view of God more present in your thoughts and prayers?

_____

_____

_____

_____

In reading Revelation's description of the throne room of God, please keep in mind that John related the completely unfamiliar through the familiar. Imagine, for example, escorting an Indian who had never ventured farther than the most primitive part of the Amazon through a tour of the state-of-the-art technology at NASA. When he returned to his fellow tribesmen, how would he describe jets or rockets? He'd probably have to begin his illustration by using birds as an example and try to stretch their imagination from there. Likewise, throughout much of Revelation, John employed known concepts to express images beyond our understanding. The throne of God is simply beyond anything we can imagine.

Yet Hebrews 4:14–16 says that because of Jesus, our great High Priest, we can approach His throne with confidence. No, none of us is without sin (1 John 1:8), but because Christ has become our atoning sacrifice, we need never fear approaching God with our confessions. He wants us to "receive mercy and find grace to help us" in our need (Heb. 4:16).

In the imagery of the throne room, I like to imagine God the Father catching those confessions in the palm of His mighty hand and casting them into the sea. What sea? Perhaps the one most conveniently located right in front of His throne. No matter how many confessions are made, this sea is never muddied by our sins. Rather, as God casts them into the sea, I like to imagine our sins instantly bleached into utter non-existence, swallowed in the depths of crystal-clear waters.

When it comes to dealing with your past sins, are you a deep-sea fisherman? Are you tempted by guilt, condemnation, and unbelief to dredge up old sins and agonize over them? Satan constantly volunteers to be our fishing guide. He even provides a handy lure to cause us to doubt God's forgiveness. How successful has he been with you?

I certainly have done some deep-sea fishing in my lifetime. But what a waste of time and energy—because when we're fishing in the right sea, our line will always come up bare. Anything we think we're seeing on the end of that line is a vain imagination. We won't even catch an old boot. Let's consider giving the enemy one instead.

PRAYING GOD'S WORD TODAY

O God, You have promised in Your Word that You will forgive our wrongdoing and never again remember our sin (Jer. 31:34), that it is You who sweep away transgressions—for Your own sake (Isa. 43:25). What incredible mercy! What amazing grace! Your love has not only delivered me from the pit of destruction, but You have thrown all my sins behind Your back (Isa. 38:17). May I walk with my head up in this air of freedom that You have created around me and within me. I am holy and righteous in Your sight, fully accepted. It's as clear as crystal in Your Word. Hallelujah!

DAY 78

The Throne of God

Before You Begin

Read Revelation 4:6b–11

Stop and Consider

The 24 elders fall down before the One seated on the throne, worship the One who lives forever and ever, [and] cast their crowns before the throne. (v. 10)

Do you live as if God—the blessed and only Ruler, the King of kings and the Lord of lords (1 Tim. 6:15)—is perfectly able to manage Your life and Your problems? If not, why not?

_____

_____

How do we keep our "crowns"—our achievements, responsibilities, things that make up our own unique identities—cast before the throne, before His feet, at their rightful place?

_____

_____

_____

Much of humanity's trouble stems from our naturally insatiable self-centeredness. We often see ourselves as the center of the universe and tend to describe all other components in reference to us rather than God. The human psyche almost invariably processes incoming information in relationship to its own ego. For example, if the news forecasts an economic slump, the natural hearer automatically processes what it could mean to self, how it affects me, my family, my situation in life.

While this response is natural, in perpetual practice this self-absorption is miserable. In some ways our egocentrism is a secret lust for omnipotence. We want to be our own god and have all power.

Our first reaction upon hearing this bit of truth might be to deny it—that we've never had a desire to be God. But how often do we take immediate responsibility for handling most of the problems in our midst? How often do we try changing the people we know and feeding our control addiction with the drug of manipulation? Simply put, we try to play God, and frankly, it's exhausting.

But thankfully, those of us who are redeemed are also given what 1 Corinthians 2:16 calls the "mind of Christ." Life takes on a far more accurate estimation and perspective when we learn to view it increasingly through the vantage point of the One who spoke it into existence.

Think of some of your greatest challenges. Picture them. Then go back and stamp the words "before the throne" in front each of these challenges.

The heart of prayer is moving these very kinds of tests and trials from the insecurities and uncertainties of earth to the throne of God. Only then can they be viewed with dependable accuracy and boundless hope. Close your eyes and do your best to picture the glorious seraphim never ceasing to cry, "Holy, holy, holy!" Imagine the lightning emitting from the throne, and hear the rumblings and the thunder. Picture the elders overwhelmed by God's worthiness, casting their crowns before the throne. Approach the throne of grace with confidence, with eyes on Him, not on yourself. Our God is huge! Our God is able!

PRAYING GOD'S WORD TODAY

You reign, Lord! You are robed in majesty, enveloped in strength. Your throne has been established from the beginning; You are from eternity. Oh yes, the floods have lifted their voices; they've lifted up their pounding waves. But greater than the roar of many waters and the mighty breakers of the sea—You, Lord, You are on high and You are majestic. Your testimonies are completely reliable. Holiness is the beauty of Your house for all the days to come (Ps. 93:1–5). I put my total trust in Your keeping strength.

DAY 79

Depth of Emotion

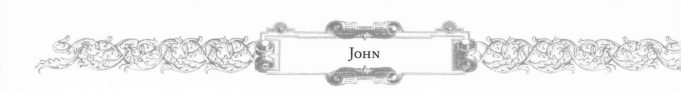
BEFORE YOU BEGIN

Read Revelation 5:1–4

STOP AND CONSIDER

I cried and cried because no one was found worthy
to open the scroll or even to look in it. (v. 4)

Some people want to take all the emotion out of Christian faith, but why is this an incomplete view of godly living? How have you experienced emotion in your walk with Christ?

_____

_____

What types of things should bring tears to our eyes? As we look around at our world and see it through the eyes of Christ, what should grieve us enough to weep before the Lord?

_____

_____

_____

We can't be certain what the scroll represents. One possibility is that it is like the one in Ezekiel's vision (Ezek. 2:9–10). That scroll contained words of lament and woe. Certainly the coming chapters announce woes, so the interpretation is plausible for the Revelation 5:1 scroll. But when Christ victoriously claims the scroll, the eruptions of praise cause me to wonder how the scroll can be associated with woes and laments alone. I tend to think the seals themselves involve wrath, but the words within unfold something glorious.

Interpreters pose another possibility—that the scroll represented the will or testament of God concerning the completion of all things on earth and the transition to all things in heaven. The ancient Romans sealed wills or testaments with six seals. A slight variation of this view compares the scene to the Roman law of inheritance. Some scholars believe the scroll is the title deed to earth.

It's all very interesting. And though I'm curious, I am comfortable not knowing the exact identity of the scroll because, whatever it is, it is in the hands of Christ. But I am touched beyond measure by John's response to what happens in verses 2 and 3, when the angel asks if anyone is "worthy to open the scroll and to break its seals." These events may not have happened over a simple matter of seconds. The verb tense of the Greek word for "proclaiming" may suggest the mighty angel could have repeated the question several times, scattering glances to and fro for someone who was worthy. The deafening silence that occurred when no one was able to answer the question only heightened the anxiety of those present. It certainly did for John. He himself admits that he "cried and cried."

His weeping reminds us that the power and presence of the Holy Spirit doesn't make us feel less. The Spirit brings life. Every one of John's senses was surely quickened by what he saw and heard. His response to the sight of the throne must have been indescribable awe. When he heard the angelic proclamation, a tidal wave of grief crashed against that reverent backdrop. Yet John was not too big a man to show both ends of this emotional spectrum. I like that about him.

Praying God's Word Today

Lord, Your Word speaks prophetically of a time when young and old—the aged, the children, even those nursing at the breast—the bridegroom and the bride coming from their honeymoon chamber—all gather together as the priests weep between the portico and the altar, saying, "Have pity on Your people, Lord" (Joel 2:16–17). We are dependent upon You as our Savior, Lord Christ. We weep at the thought that You—the only One worthy—have redeemed our fallen souls. We long to feel every emotion associated with such grace, hope, and mercy. Thank You, Lord.

DAY 80

The Lamb

BEFORE YOU BEGIN

Read Revelation 5:5–14

STOP AND CONSIDER

Blessing and honor and glory and dominion to the One
seated on the throne, and to the Lamb, forever and ever! (v. 13)

What makes this image of "the Lamb" so compelling and complete? Why do you think
God chose it to represent His Son's sacrifice for our sins? _____

_____

_____

Think of some more words that belong in this list of praises ascribed to the "One seated on
the throne and to the Lamb." Blessing, honor, glory, dominion, and . . . _____

_____

_____

_____

Genesis 1:24–25 tells of the creation of animal life. In the midst of countless creatures, hoofed and not, God created the lamb. I happen to think God is the sentimental type. It shows throughout Scripture, and we as sentimental people were created in His image. I don't think He created the lamb with little notice. He knew the profound significance He would cause this small, helpless creature to have. Adam wasn't created until after the animals. God saved what He considered His best for last. But I think the fact that a lamb was created before a man is quite fitting because throughout the Old Testament, man would require a heap of them.

After sin cost Adam and Eve paradise, "the LORD God made clothing out of skins for Adam and his wife, and He clothed them" (Gen. 3:21). This is the first reference to a sacrificial death. Since God dressed them with a skin, we know an animal perished for them to be covered. We have no way of knowing whether the animal was a lamb, but I can hardly picture it any other way.

Genesis 4:4 records the first sacrificial offering. "Abel also presented an offering—some of the firstborn of his flock and their fat portions." Cain brought an offering of fruit, but the Lord looked with favor on Abel's offering.

Not coincidentally, from the moment in Scripture that life appears outside the garden, we see sacrificial offerings. God wasn't partial to Abel. He was partial to Abel's offering. When not distinguished otherwise, a flock almost always refers to sheep in Scripture. From the Old Testament to the New, the Lord looks with favor upon those symbolically covered by the blood of the Lamb. Verse 7 hints that Cain knew the right thing to do and had the same chance to bring a sacrificial offering. The basic tenet of all biblical rebellion is refusing the blood of the lamb.

Genesis 22 contains the account of Abraham's willingness to sacrifice his son Isaac in obedience to God. Far from coincidence, the first time in Scripture the word "lamb" is used is in Genesis 22. Fittingly, the words "sacrifice" and "worship" are introduced in the same chapter, and the word "love" appears for only the second time.

Just before Abraham actually killed his son as an offering to God, the angel of the Lord intervened. God provided a substitute sacrifice in the form of a ram caught in the thicket. I was thrilled when I read the following definition of *ayil*, the word for "ram": "a male sheep

> We hang our heads over the sad estate of this world. And all the while God sits upon His throne saying, "As long as man has breath, I have a Lamb."

generally more aggressive and protective of the flock." Jesus our Lamb is indeed aggressively protective of the flock—even to the spilling of His blood. Galatians calls this drama the gospel preached in advance to Abraham (Gal. 3:8; Rom. 9:7). Glory!

We cannot find a more perfect Old Testament picture of the blood of the sacrificial lamb than the one that's recorded in Exodus 12. The final plague against Egypt came in the form of the death of the firstborn. Every Hebrew family found protection through the Passover lamb's blood on the doorpost.

So the concept of substitutionary atonement that unfolded immediately outside the Garden of Eden echoed like a sermon from Isaac's Mt. Moriah, dripped from the doorposts of captive Israel, and remained constant throughout the Old Testament. Innumerable animals were sacrificed throughout the centuries at the altars of the tabernacle and the temple. So many were sacrificed at the dedication of Solomon's temple that they couldn't be counted.

Yet Israel repeatedly fell into idolatry. And after sending the prophets with warnings, Old Testament Scripture comes to an abrupt halt—but not without a promise: "Look, I am going to send you Elijah the prophet before the great and awesome Day of the LORD comes" (Mal. 4:5). According to Matthew 11:12–14, John the Baptist fulfilled this prophecy. Look at the first words from John the Baptist's mouth when he saw Jesus: "Here is the Lamb of God, who takes away the sin of the world!" (John 1:29).

Luke 22 records the last supper Christ shared with His disciples. Because a Jewish day begins just after sundown and lasts until the next, Christ was actually crucified on the very same "day" they ate their final meal together. According to Luke 22:14 that day was when Jesus' hour had come.

Oh, do you realize we've only seen a glimpse, yet look at the consistency! A lamb, the lamb, the Lamb! So that we wouldn't miss the woolen thread, this book of the Bible that brings all things to completion shouts this title like triumphant bursts from a ram's horn. Not once. Not twice. But twenty-eight times! The Lamb slain from the foundation of the world for the salvation of the world.

Man can shake his arrogant fist all he wants, but he will never shake God. The plan is firm. No plan B exists. All things are going just as He knew they would. We look around us and hang our heads over the miserable estate of this lost, depraved world. And all the while God sits upon His throne saying, "As long as man has breath, I have a Lamb."

When you see this consistent theme of "the Lamb" running so strong and true throughout the long corridor of Scripture, how secure do you feel in His eternal love for you, extending back farther than the foundation of the world? You should. The Lamb is slain for you.

_____

_____

_____

_____

_____

_____

PRAYING GOD'S WORD TODAY

Your grace has appeared, Lord, with salvation for all people, instructing us to deny godlessness and worldly lusts and to live in a sensible, righteous, and godly way in the present age, while we wait for the blessed hope and the appearing of the glory of our great God and Savior, Jesus Christ. You gave Yourself for us to redeem us from all lawlessness and to cleanse for Yourself a special people, eager to do good works (Titus 2:11–14). I worship You today, Lamb of God, with words and actions that express my heartfelt appreciation.

DAY 81

Learning a New Song

Before You Begin

Read Revelation 14:1–5

Stop and Consider

They sang a new song before the throne . . . but no one could learn the song
except the 144,000 who had been redeemed from the earth. (v. 3)

Do you have a testimony about a time when God gave you a new song or a new hope in a
virtually hopeless situation? Call it to mind again. What do you most remember about it?

_____

_____

What are some of the "songs"—whether actual titles or pivotal truths—that have ministered to you in times of deep need? _____

_____

_____

_____

I am not a singer, but I dearly love to sing praise songs to my God. My favorite songs are the ones that become "mine" over time as I sing them to God through the filter of my own experience and affection.

Nothing provokes a new song in my heart like a fresh surge of hope in a wilderness season. The song "Shout to the Lord" will forever be special to me because I first heard it at a time of deep personal suffering. The words came to my soul from God as hope that I would survive . . . and even thrive once again. Allow me to use this song as an illustration for Revelation 14:3. First I "heard" the new song, then I "learned" it. My motivation to "learn" it came through its voice to my experience in that difficult but strangely beautiful season with my God.

John "heard" the new song, but "no one could learn the song" except the 144,000 who had been redeemed from the earth. The Greek word for "new" in reference to the new song in Revelation 14:3 implies new in quality as opposed to number. In other words, the song wasn't new like a new release. The song of the 144,000 was "new" because it had an entirely different quality from anything they'd sung before. In other words, it meant something to them no other song had ever meant. Why couldn't anyone else learn it? Because no one else had ever lived it. Out of their unique experience, God gave them a song that only they could learn.

Psalm 40 tells us God gave David a new song when He lifted him out of the slimy pit. I'd like to suggest that each of us who is willing can also receive a new song from God that arises in our souls out of hardship's victories—not necessarily in musical notes but in fresh truths engraved on the heart. These are precious gifts that eventually come to those who keep the faith and wait to see God redeem great difficulty. These songs can be "heard" by others, but they cannot be "learned" secondhand. Songs of the heart are only learned through personal faith experience—through hurts, losses, and failures that have been handed over to Jesus to heal and transform. And once we learn the songs, no one can take them from us.

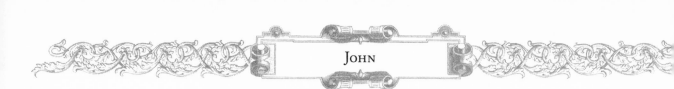

PRAYING GOD'S WORD TODAY

You send Your faithful love by day, and Your song is with me in the night—a prayer to the God of my life (Ps. 42:8). I sing it to You now, just the way You've taught it to me . . .

DAY 82

His Righteous Wrath

BEFORE YOU BEGIN

Read Revelation 15:1–8

STOP AND CONSIDER

Then I saw another great and awe-inspiring sign in heaven: seven angels with the seven last plagues, for with them, God's wrath will be completed. (v. 1)

The wrath of God is an uncomfortable concept. But what does it tell us about Him? _____

_____

_____

Knowing human nature as you do, what would our world be like if not for a fear of God?

_____

_____

_____

_____

Perhaps the truest words that ever fall from tainted human lips are these: God is faithful. Indeed He is. What may trouble us is that He is *always* faithful. In other words, God always does what He insists He will whether we like it or not.

The idealist in me wishes the wrath of God didn't even exist and would never be unleashed. Then the realist in me . . .

- reads accounts of unspeakable cruelties and abuses to children;
- reviews a human history blighted by war crimes and bloody crusades;
- hears the name of God mocked, profaned, and publicly derided;
- listens to the arrogant who have convinced themselves they are gods;
- sees the violence bred by hatred, ignorance, and prejudice;
- watches princes of the earth lay bricks on an unseen but very present Tower of Babel.

I look around me and shudder with horror over and over again, asking, "Where is the fear of God?" Then I shake my head and wonder what kind of inconceivable power God must use to restrain Himself.

I don't even have to look as far as the world. At times in my life I've looked no further than my own mirror or my own church and wondered the words of Lamentations 3:22 (NIV), "Because of the Lord's great love we are not consumed." I have said to Him more times than I can count, "Lord, why You do not rend this earth and swallow up Your own people, not to mention this godless world, is beyond me." Why does God continue to put up with a world that increasingly mocks Him? Why does He wait? For all of time, the most succinct answer to those questions can be found in 2 Peter 3:9: "The Lord does not delay His promise, as some understand delay, but is patient with you, not wanting any to perish, but all to come to repentance."

In some ways the wrath of God will simply finish off what man has started. I am convinced that mankind will do a proficient job of nearly destroying himself and his own planet based on the wars and conflicts prophesied in Scripture. God's Word promises a new heaven and a new earth but not until this one is destroyed. Matthew 24 prophesies increasing wickedness and destruction with a mounting strength and frequency of birth pains. Toward the very end of this age, God will allow the full measure of all permissible wrath to be poured out upon this earth: the wrath of man (never underestimate it), the unholy wrath of Satan, and the holy wrath of God. No wonder this time of great tribulation will be like no other.

The wrath described in the book of Revelation unfolds in a somewhat mysterious sequence: seals, trumpets, and bowls. The seals introduce the trumpets, and the trumpets usher in the bowls. To call this "unsettling" is an understatement. My horror is primarily for those who refuse to believe, of course, because in 1 Thessalonians 1:10, Paul called Jesus the one "who rescues us from the coming wrath."

I am not implying that believers won't go through terrible times. The Word clearly states we will (2 Tim. 3:1), and many Christians already are. My point is that the wrath of God described in the book of Revelation is not toward the redeemed. They will either be delivered *from* it or *through* it.

Inoculation against the wrath of God is confessing His Son as Savior and repenting of sin. No one who comes to Him with a heart of repentance will be refused.

God will reveal Himself in countless ways toward the end of times, pouring out His Spirit, His wonders, and His mercies. Those mercies, however, are dealt according to demand. In other words, some people respond to *tender* mercies. Others don't respond until God shows *severe* mercies. Others don't respond at all. Never forget that God wants to save people and not destroy them. During the last days, the heavens will show so many signs, and evangelists will preach so powerfully that I am convinced people will practically have to work at refusing Him. Yet many tragically will.

The apostle Paul warned that "because of your hardness and unrepentant heart you are storing up wrath for yourself in the day of wrath, when God's righteous judgment is revealed" (Rom. 2:5). People will not refuse Him because God didn't love them or make provision for them. Beloved, please hear my heart. The wrath of God cannot be separated from His character and person. In other words, even in His unleashed wrath, God cannot be less than who He is. God is holy. He is good. He is love. God is righteous, and God is right. The Judge will judge, but His judgments are always based on truth (Rom. 2:2).

Ours is also a God of inconceivable compassion, forgiveness, and mercy. God's heart is neither mean nor unjust. He is holy. And beloved, the holy God will judge this world. The day of the Lord will come, and none will doubt He is God. He will not be mocked. He'd have to be untrue to His own character to do otherwise.

This is serious, no doubt about it. Since the Bible is true, we know many people who—if unwilling to receive Christ as Savior—are on a collision course with unspeakable, unending woes. Think of some of these dear ones you know. They don't need a namby-pamby God. How can you show Him to be strong through your life and testimony? _____

_____

_____

_____

_____

_____

_____

PRAYING GOD'S WORD TODAY

Let no one deceive us, Lord, with empty arguments. Your wrath is definitely coming on the disobedient (Eph. 5:6). Their silver and their gold will not be able to rescue them on the day of Your wrath. Your Word says the whole earth will be consumed by the fire of Your jealousy. For You will make a complete, yes, a horrifying end of all the inhabitants of the earth (Zeph. 1:18). But since we have now been declared righteous by Christ's blood, we will be saved through Him from wrath (Rom. 5:9). May this realization drive me to daring acts of spiritual rescue for my unsaved friends and family, and drive me to my knees in grateful, genuine praise.

DAY 83

Come Wearing White

Before You Begin
Read Revelation 19:1–10

Stop and Consider
The marriage of the Lamb has come, and His wife has prepared herself.
She was permitted to wear fine linen, bright and pure. (vv. 7–8)

I'm telling you, this is great news to me and to all who have a difficult background or track
record. Think of it—"fine linen, bright and pure." How does it feel to have that on? _____

_____

_____

Satan, though, hates the way you look in white. And he'll do anything in the world to keep
you from wearing it. How is he trying right now to keep you feeling less than pure? _____

_____

_____

_____

As I was preparing for our twentieth wedding anniversary, for the life of me I could not think of what I wanted to get my husband. He's a very sentimental man. You have to get him something sentimental because if he can afford it, he already owns anything he wants. So I just said, "God, you need to tell me what I can get my man. I need a really great idea." Honestly, I prayed and prayed over this. Then God began suggesting something to my heart.

He started bringing to my mind the early part of our marriage and the pain of my wedding day. I don't know how to explain this to you, but trust me when I say that it was an extremely hard day for me. I didn't really understand why until many, many years later. I was feeling so much shame on my wedding day because it was a day I was supposed to feel beautiful. And I did not feel beautiful.

I had even gone to a lot of trouble to make absolutely sure that I had an off-white dress instead of a white one, because I didn't want to be a lie. Some of you are already hurting because you know what I'm talking about. It's a horrible feeling. Nothing about that day seemed beautiful to me.

When I was a little girl, I had pictured that when I got married I would have a huge wedding portrait, and it would hang over our blazing fireplace. Well, the nearest thing we had to a fireplace was a heater in the bathroom. And I didn't even have money enough for a photographer. I just spent the bare minimum. I didn't even buy my dress; I just rented it. You know, it just was not the kind of day you picture.

So as I contemplated our twentieth anniversary, the Lord began scratching at this a little bit. He said, "You know, Beth," and of course He was speaking to my heart, "you never did get that picture made."

"What picture?"

"That wedding portrait."

"Well, it's a little too late now, isn't it?"

"Who said?"

The Lord put it on my heart that it was time. He said, "My darlin', we have done so much work. I have restored you. And it is time for you to put on a white wedding gown and get your picture taken for your husband."

So I called a friend of mine who's a makeup artist in Houston, a very godly young woman. I knew she would have a fit. She squealed on the phone and jumped up and down. I said, "You can't tell anyone, Shannon. This is our secret." She said, "I'll set up everything. You just show up and I'll have it all ready." That's exactly what I did. And I'm going to tell you something, she hid me in a room and would not let me see a mirror. She had my dress sparkling white from head to toe. Zipped that thing up nice and tight. Did my makeup. Did my hair. Put on my veil. Then she pulled me out and brought me in front of the mirror. And I nearly died.

As we grow in Christ, we become more and more beautiful to the One for whom we're preparing ourselves. We are preparing for our wedding day.

I couldn't even recognize myself. The photographer was so tender that his eyes were continually filled with tears. He said, "I've got to be honest with you. I've never taken a picture of a bride this old." Sheepishly catching his *faux pas*, he said, "That's not what I mean—I mean one that's been married for so long." He was right. This was a forty-one-year-old bride who had been married for twenty years.

I had the picture placed in the most ornate gold frame, 20 x 24. Then I had one made for each of my daughters. I wrote the same letter to Keith and the girls, explaining what the portrait meant to me.

The night of our anniversary, I had the girls stay with us, and I presented Keith with this picture, then presented their pictures to them. They all read their letters at the same time. My husband began to weep. He stood up with that picture, and he began walking all over the house, holding it up to places on the wall.

He would stop at one place and shake his head no, then stop at another and shake his head no. Finally he walked right over to a particular part of the wall. The girls and I caught our breath because we knew what he was looking at. He set the picture down. Then gathering his courage, he pulled his trophy deer off the wall.

As I live and breathe, he had tears streaming down his cheeks, and I thought, "He's crying over that deer." But he hung that picture up right there, and it still hangs there today. He stepped back and said, "That is the trophy of my life." A restored bride. And that is what every single one of us can be—fully restored, fully prepared. For our Groom.

Take a moment to remind yourself how your Bridegroom sees you—not the way you may imagine it, but the way His Word says it—"enthralled by your beauty" (Ps. 45:11 NIV).

PRAYING GOD'S WORD TODAY

Lord, Your Word says that I will be presented to you as a pure virgin (2 Cor. 11:2)—in splendor, without spot or wrinkle or any such thing, but holy and blameless (Eph. 5:27). My head spins. My body trembles. My spirit soars. I am pure before You—pure because of You—washed for all eternity in Your cleansing blood. Hallelujah, Lord Jesus!

DAY 84

A Heavenly Sight

BEFORE YOU BEGIN

Read Revelation 19:11–21

STOP AND CONSIDER

Then I saw heaven opened, and there was a white horse! Its rider is called
Faithful and True, and in righteousness He judges and makes war. (v. 11)

What other name could be quite so descriptive of Christ as "Faithful and True"? How has
He lived up to these titles in the past few weeks and months? _____

_____

_____

What do you need Him to declare war against in your own life? What battles are you
trying to wage on your own, while the righteous Judge stands ready to mount the attack?

_____

_____

_____

When I first wrote this little piece of creative writing several years ago, I really thought I understood from Revelation 19 that the wedding supper would precede Jesus' second coming. But now that I look at the text, I'm not sure of that. It could be that it comes after, but I wrote this with the first understanding. It's just a fictional writing anyway. I share the final portion of it with you just to get your mind going.

The horse's coat was white with a luster like pearls. His mane was strands of gold. His eyes were like wine. His muscles ridged under his coat, displaying his impeccable condition. The Groom stared at him with approval, then smiled with familiarity as His hand stroked his mighty neck. Two cherubim brought forth a wooden chest laden with gold and brilliant jewels. Saints covered their eyes from the blinding light as they lifted the lid. The dazzling radiance was veiled as they brought forth a crimson robe from within and placed it upon the Groom's shoulders. Gold tassels were tied around His neck, and the seraph spread forth His train. The words were embroidered in deep purple, "King of Kings and Lord of Lords." His foot went in the stirrup, and the Faithful and True mounted His horse. The beast dipped his head as if to bow, then lifted it with an inexpressible assumption of responsibility. The Groom gently tugged the reins to the right and the animal turned with exemplary obedience.

Suddenly, a sound erupted like rolling thunder. The earth rumbled beneath their feet. The walls of the banquet hall gave way with a stunning thud. And encircling them were horses no man could count, winged and ready for flight. The four creatures—one with a face like a lion, one like an ox, one like a man, and one like a flying eagle—flew over the heads of the saints and sang the anthem, "All rise!" Each saint, dressed in white linen, rose from his chair and mounted his horse. The attentions of every saint were quickened by the Groom. His back still turned. His horse made ready. Suddenly, a vapor seeped from the ground and covered the hooves of the horse of Faithful and True. As the vapor rose to His thighs, the fog became a cloud enveloping the Rider inch by inch. Brilliance overtook

Him, and He became as radiant as the sun. So great was His glory, the cloud rose to His shoulders and covered His head to shield the eyes of the saints.

The familiar surroundings of heaven were suddenly transformed, and the sky appeared

His name ascended above all names. The cloud lifted above His shoulder, and the knowledge of God was unveiled in the face of Jesus Christ.

under His feet. A deafening sound emitted from the middle of heaven like the slow rending of a heavy veil. The sky beneath their feet rolled by like a scroll, and the inhabitants of heaven were suspended in the earth's atmosphere. The planet was their destiny. The Groom was their cue. The cloudy pillar that enveloped Him would plot their course.

With swiftness the cloud descended toward the Earth. The horses behind Him kept perfect cadence. The Earth grew larger as they made their final approach, and oceans could be distinguished from the nations. The Earth turned until Jerusalem faced upward. The cloudy pillar circled widely to the right for the Rider's eastward arrival.

The sun interrupted the night as it rose upon the city of Zion and awakened every inhabitant in the land. The rays that poured through their windows were unlike those of any other morning. All who saw it sensed the imposing arrival of the supernatural. The wicked inhabitants of Jerusalem's houses, those who had forced the people of God from their homes, shielded their eyes as they filled the city streets. All of Israel was awakened, and the valleys were filled with people gazing upward as much as their vision would permit to something awesomely beyond terrestrial. Emaciated humans filtered one by one from every cave and crevice—those who had not taken the mark of the beast. Their eyes tried to adjust to such sudden and abnormal gusts of light after hiding in the darkness for so long. Every eye looked upon the amazing cloudy pillar as it made its approach just east of the city of Zion.

The cloud stopped midair.

Suddenly the divine veil began to roll upward inch by inch, exposing first only the hooves of the great white horse then the feet of the Rider. They looked like burning brass in the stirrups. His crimson robe was exposed little by little until it seemed to blanket the sky. His name ascended above all names. The cloud lifted above His shoulder, and the knowledge of God was unveiled in the face of Jesus Christ. His eyes burned like fire into every heart. Those who had taken the mark of the beast ran for their lives, shoving the people of God out of the way as they took cover in the caves. The people of God's covenant and those who had come to their aid remained in the light, entranced by the glorious sight. Moaning filled the air. The Rider on the white horse dismounted His beast, and His feet touched down on the Mount of Olives. The earth quaked with indescribable force. And all who were hiding lost their cover.

The large brown eyes of one small boy remained fixed upon the sight. The whiteness of his teeth contrasted with the filth covering his face as he broke into an inexperienced smile. He reached over and took his mother's bony hands from her face and held them gently. "Look, Mom, no more crying. Surely that is our God. We trusted in Him and He saved us." Even so, Lord Jesus, come quickly.

Your immediate reaction to this real yet somewhat imagined scene—what captures you?

_____

_____

_____

_____

Praying God's Word Today

The Spirit of the Lord rests upon You, Lord Jesus—a Spirit of wisdom and understanding, a Spirit of counsel and strength, a Spirit of knowledge and of the fear of the Lord. You do not judge by what You see with Your eyes; You do not execute justice by what You hear with Your ears, but You judge the poor righteously and execute justice for the oppressed of the land. Righteousness and faithfulness are like a belt around Your waist (Isa. 11:1–5). And we, Your people, find ourselves safe in Your strong arms. Glory to Your name, Lord Jesus. You alone are Faithful and True.

DAY 85

Link by Link

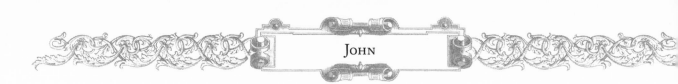
BEFORE YOU BEGIN

Read Revelation 20:1–6

STOP AND CONSIDER

I saw an angel coming down from heaven with the key to the abyss and a great
chain in his hand. He seized . . . Satan and bound him for 1,000 years. (vv. 1–2)

What would you like to shout at Satan while he sits in his little dungeon, a chain restrict-
ing him to nothing more than a toothless bark? Don't feel sorry for him. Let him have it.

_____

_____

For all of Satan's snarl and elusiveness, it just takes one little unnamed angel to capture
him. What does that tell you about his limited power—and God's limitless authority?

_____

_____

_____

What irony that there are references to a "great chain" and being "set free" right here in passages prophesying the devil's future. Scholars are very divided over the meaning of the 1,000-year time reference in verse 2. But no matter the time frame, Satan will be bound. That's all that matters.

And I for one couldn't be happier that the means the Lord uses to bind him is a great chain. How appropriate! Some may wonder why God will bother chaining him for a time rather than simply casting him immediately into the lake of fire. Beloved, as far as I'm concerned, the last days will be high time for Satan to be bound in chains! For all of us who have cried, "How long, O Sovereign Lord, until You avenge our bondage?" we will be able to enjoy watching him see how chains feel. In fact, I hope the "great chain" is made from all the ones that have fallen off our ankles!

I want Satan to experience the same sense of powerlessness with which he deceived many of us—the same powerlessness we felt when seeing others who were free yet not knowing for the life of us how to become one of them. Praise God for truth that sets us free! Satan tried his hardest to keep me bound and to destroy my life, my family, my testimony, and my ministry, but God defeated him by the power of His outstretched arm. The future will show Satan not only defeated but his wickedness toward us avenged. I suspect you feel the same way, that you share my glee at seeing him get what he has coming to him—and more!

What will the world be like while Satan is in chains? Based on my own personal study of last things, I tend to think the period of Satan's bondage in the abyss coincides with the kingdom of Christ on earth, a kingdom characterized by peace, righteousness, and security. Keep in mind, however, that faithful students of God's Word see a variety of ways to understand the passage. God will accomplish His will in His own way regardless of opinion. But when all is done, we will probably all stand with our mouths open in wonder.

And Satan, well—his mouth we won't have to worry about anymore.

PRAYING GOD'S WORD TODAY

I'll admit, Lord, I like the thought of Satan tossed into the abyss with the key thrown away on that day when You punish the host of heaven above and kings of the earth below. Your Word promises that they will be gathered together like prisoners in a pit, confined to a dungeon, and after many days they will be punished. The moon will be put to shame and the sun disgraced, because You will reign as king on Mount Zion in Jerusalem, and You will display Your glory in the presence of Your elders (Isa. 24:21–23). I thank You for the assured demise of the Devil, and the certain freedom of us former captives.

DAY 86

A Dark Day at
the Great White Throne

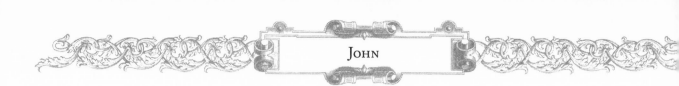
BEFORE YOU BEGIN

Read Revelation 20:7–15

STOP AND CONSIDER

Then I saw a great white throne and One seated on it.

Earth and heaven fled from His presence, and no place was found for them. (v. 11)

Knowing John as you do, try to imagine his reaction to the finality of this scene. What do you think was going through his mind at the revelation of it? _____

_____

_____

Ezekiel 33:11 reveals that God takes no pleasure in this task, in the death of the wicked. His desire is for them to turn to Him. How does that desire show itself in your heart?

_____

_____

_____

Based on my understanding of Scripture and the final judgments, only the lost will stand at the great white throne. This seat of judgment seems to differ from the one described in both 1 Corinthians 3:10–15 and 2 Corinthians 5:1–10. Those who know Christ will stand before the judgment seat of Christ where those who have served Him lovingly and obediently will receive rewards. The judgment seat for the saved will not be a place of condemnation (Rom. 8:1).

Our passages in Revelation, however, describe a very different scene. The great white throne appears to be a seat upon which only condemnation takes place. Every person who has refused God will stand before Him on this dreadful day. Though the earth and sky will try to flee from His awesome presence, those who have refused God will have no place to run. I am convinced, in fact, that Revelation 20:13 suggests differing levels of punishment according to the depths and lengths of the evil accomplished by each person. Why would I have ever thought otherwise? Is our God not just? Does He not look upon the individual hearts and deeds of every responsible man and woman? The lake of fire will be a place of torment for every inhabitant, but I believe Scripture clearly teaches that punishment will vary according to each person's deeds. The Righteous Judge knows every thought, and He rightly discerns every motive of our hearts.

Though planet Earth now bulges with billions of people, God still breathes life into each being, one at a time. We were fashioned for God and designed to seek Him. He created a universe and an order with the divine purpose of bearing constant witness to His existence. Heaven unceasingly declares His glory, and all who truly seek Him find Him.

Not one person's absence from heaven will go unnoticed by God. Not one will get past God haphazardly. Not one will accidentally get swept away in a sea of nameless souls. God is not careless. He intimately knows every soul that will refuse to know Him. Because He created us for fellowship, God's judgments cannot be rendered with cold, sterile detachment. For God so loved the world that He sent His Son to seek and to save the lost. Though none can refuse to be seen, many will incomprehensibly refuse to be "found."

PRAYING GOD'S WORD TODAY

Lord, I grieve at the thought of those who will stand defenseless before Your righteous judgment, unable to avoid Your presence, though they avoided You at every opportunity on earth. It makes me long all the more to draw near You each moment of the day, to see Your face in righteousness, and when I awake from sleep, to be satisfied with Your presence (Ps. 17:15).

DAY 87

Back Home Again

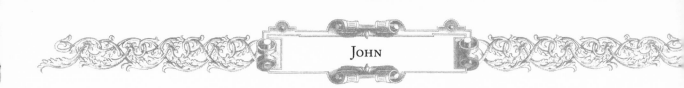

BEFORE YOU BEGIN

Read Revelation 21:1–8

STOP AND CONSIDER

I also saw the Holy City, new Jerusalem, coming down out of heaven
from God, prepared like a bride adorned for her husband. (v. 2)

Who or what has been taken from you in this life that you fully expect God to restore to
you when you enter the gates of the heavenly city? _____

_____

_____

What blighted and unkempt parts of our society grieve your heart the most, making you
long for a totally renewed, totally restored, totally perfect homeland? _____

_____

_____

I am confident that most of us Gentiles cannot relate to the attachment many Jews through the centuries have felt toward their homeland. Even those whose feet never touched the Holy Land yearned for it like a lost child longs for its mother.

I saw this peculiar bond just weeks ago in the face of my Hebrew friend and ancient lands guide, Arie. He and his family are now residents of Tel Aviv, but his heart never departs Jerusalem. The turmoil erupting within and around Jerusalem doesn't just concern or upset him. It brings him pain. I asked him how he felt about the ongoing crises in the Holy Land. As I witnessed the agony in his face, I sorrowed that I had asked something so obviously intimate. I consider myself very patriotic, yet I had to acknowledge that I knew nothing of his attachment to his own homeland.

If Arie and other Jews through the ages have experienced an indescribable attachment to the Holy City, try to imagine the strength of John's ties. He grew up on the shores of Galilee at the peak of Jerusalem's splendor since the days of Solomon. Herod's temple was one of the greatest wonders of John's world. No Jew could behold her splendor without marveling. Even weeping.

John knew every wall and gate of the Holy City. He walked the lengths and breadths with the Savior Himself. He sat near Him on the Mount of Olives, overlooking its beauty. John was also part of the generation who witnessed the total destruction in AD 70. By the time Jerusalem fell, John probably was already stationed in Ephesus, but the news traveled fast, and the sobs echoed louder with every mile. The grief of the diaspora mixed with the unreasonable guilt of not having died with the city surely shook their homesick souls.

Then how his heart must have leapt upon seeing the new Jerusalem! There it was! Not just restored but created anew with splendor beyond compare. I wonder if John was weeping at the sight. Some people say that we won't be able to cry in the new heavens and earth. Clearly we get at least one last good cry, though, since God will wipe away every tear! I cannot imagine that I will see my Christ, my God, and His heavenly kingdom with dry eyes. Our last tears, however, will no longer be those shed in mourning.

PRAYING GOD'S WORD TODAY

Thank You, Lord, for looking down from Your holy heights, for gazing out from heaven to earth to hear a prisoner's groaning, to set free those condemned to die, so that we might declare Your name in Zion and Your praise in Jerusalem when peoples and kingdoms are assembled to serve You (Ps. 102:19–22). I can't wait—to see it, to see You, to praise You!

DAY 88

Your Name Here

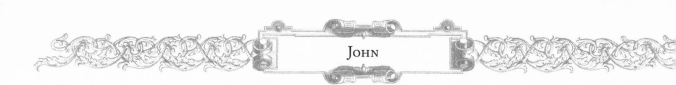
Before You Begin

Read Revelation 21:9–21

Stop and Consider

The city wall had 12 foundations, and on them
were the 12 names of the Lamb's 12 apostles. (v. 14)

What lessons do you draw from the fact that this heavenly city is so carefully constructed, laid out with such clear intention and precision? _____

_____

_____

What about the radiant beauty of it? Yes, the city is tightly measured, and yet it shimmers in opulent glory. What does this tell you about our God? _____

_____

_____

_____

Throughout our various looks at Revelation over these many days and weeks, we have preoccupied ourselves with what John saw, beginning with the moment a loud voice sounded behind him like a trumpet, saying, "Write on a scroll what you see." Let's now take one last glimpse at a detail in the new Jerusalem that might have had a fairly profound impact on John—the sight of the heavenly city's foundations, upon which were written the names of the twelve apostles.

Beloved, do you realize that among them John saw his own name? In the days he remained on this earth, can you imagine what kinds of thoughts he had as he recaptured that sight in his memory? I have no idea what being one of Jesus' apostles was like, but I don't think they felt superhuman or vaguely worthy of their calling. I'm not even sure those original disciples ever grasped that what they were doing would make a world-changing impact. I can't picture them thinking, "What I'm doing this moment will go down in history and be recorded in the eternal annals of glory." I think they probably got down on themselves just like you and I do. I also think they were terribly overwhelmed at the prospect of reaching their world with the gospel of Christ and seeing only handfuls of converts most of the time.

Days and months later, when John stared at that wall and its foundations again in his memory, can't you imagine he was nearly overcome that God esteemed them? Don't you think he marveled that the plan had worked . . . considering the mortal agents Christ had chosen to use?

Every day I deal with a measure of low self-esteem in ministry. I never feel up to the task. Never smart enough. Never strong enough. Never prayed up enough. Never prepared enough. Do you feel the same way? Then perhaps you also feel the same flood of emotions when this truth washes over you: God loves us. He prepares an inconceivable place for those who receive His love. He highly esteems those who choose to believe His call over the paralyzing screams of their own insecurities. No, our names won't be written on the foundations of the new Jerusalem, but they are engraved in the palms of His hands.

PRAYING GOD'S WORD TODAY

No, may I never say, "The Lord has abandoned me; The Lord has forgotten me!" For You Yourself have said, "Can a woman forget her nursing child, or lack compassion for the child of her womb? Even if these forget, yet I will not forget you. Look, I have inscribed you on the palms of My hands; your walls are continually before Me" (Isa. 49:14–16). Even when I don't feel like it, help me know that the place where I stand with You—because of the merits of Your grace and the atoning work of Christ—is a place of love and honor.

DAY 89

All You Ever Wanted

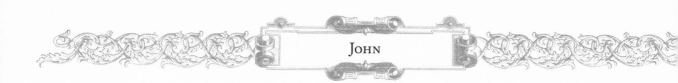
BEFORE YOU BEGIN

Read Revelation 21:22–27

STOP AND CONSIDER

I did not see a sanctuary in it, because the Lord God
the Almighty and the Lamb are its sanctuary. (v. 22)

What are some of the visual elements in your own church that represent the presence of
God in your midst? _____

_____

_____

I'm thankful for these—the cross, the Communion table, the various tools that keep us
reminded of Him. But imagine seeing Him with your own eyes! What would you do?

_____

_____

_____

Seven blessings are pronounced during a Jewish wedding ceremony, each of which comes from the dignitaries at the wedding, my friend Arie tells me. Usually the rabbi begins it. Then maybe a father-in-law, maybe an uncle, maybe an older brother. But there are seven blessings spoken. And the seventh blessing is always the blessing over Jerusalem. I find this to be very intriguing. The blessing goes something like this: "Bless You, Lord, the Builder of Jerusalem, who will rebuild the temple one day."

Then what do you suppose they do? What is the part you and I probably know the best? Right—they break the glass.

Arie said, "There are some who think that the broken glass just begins the great ceremony, but that is not what it's about. The breaking of the glass is to bring them to a very sober time of thinking that in the midst of great celebration, we must remember"—and I'm quoting his exact words—"that our joy is incomplete."

I said, "Okay, Arie. What makes our joy incomplete?" (Remember all the times that Christ said, "Make My joy complete"?) "What makes our joy incomplete, Arie?"

"Two things," he said. "The first thing is that some of our loved ones are missing from the wedding, those who have already died. The second one is because there is no temple for now in Jerusalem."

But for us as New Testament believers, both of those longings have been satisfied. Regarding our loved ones: those in Christ will be present at the wedding supper of the Lamb. And regarding the temple: well, no, there's not a temple in this new Jerusalem. But that's okay, "because the Lord God Almighty and the Lamb are its temple" (Rev. 21:22 NIV). Who needs a place of worship when the object of our worship is right here before us, not seen through representation and symbolism, but here for the enjoying?

Isn't that enormous? No more sadness, reflection, regret, or mourning. No more holes in our happiness—having someone who's not there to share it with, a shoe waiting to drop. No more taking worship to a level that only makes our heart ache for more. Do you understand that our joy gets to be complete, just as John had reported, just as Jesus had said?

Praying God's Word Today

As it is, Lord, we do not yet see everything subjected to You, not the way Your Word declares that it one day will be. But we do see Jesus—made lower than the angels for a short time so that by Your grace He might taste death for everyone. Now He is crowned with glory and honor because of the suffering of death (Heb. 2:8–9). And someday, I will see Him, no longer in my mind's eye but in the reality of His appearing. And then my joy will be complete.

DAY 90

Face to Face

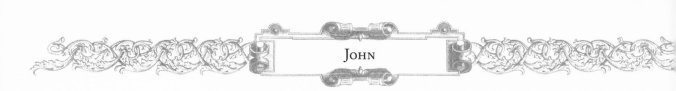
BEFORE YOU BEGIN

Read Revelation 22:1–21

STOP AND CONSIDER

I, John, am the one who heard and saw these things. (v. 8)

Among the things John saw was a river, flowing from the throne of God. How deeply do you see yourself in the figurative river of Christ's power and activity? _____

_____

_____

Do not be discouraged if you're not much more than waist deep. But are you progressing? That's the real question. We're moving toward a time when we will see Him face-to-face. How is He growing you along the way? _____

_____

_____

_____

Face-to-face. I can't think of a more fitting focus for our last few moments together. I don't want you to miss the most beautiful statement in the final chapter of Scripture: "They will see His face" (Rev. 22:4). For many of us, the very sight of Christ's face will be heaven enough. Everything else is the river overflowing its banks.

Until then we who are redeemed are like spirit-people wrapped in prison walls of flesh. Our view is impaired by the steel bars of mortal vision. We are not unlike Moses, who experienced God's presence but could not see His face. To him and to all confined momentarily by mortality, God has said, "You cannot see My face, for no one can see Me and live" (Exod. 33:20).

When all is said and done, we who are alive in Christ will indeed see His face and live. Happily ever after. I can hardly wait!

Yet right this moment I am absorbed by the thought of someone else seeing that face. Someone I've grown to love and appreciate so deeply through the months of study for this book. Several of the early church fathers plant the apostle John back in the soil of Ephesus again after the conclusion of his exile on the Island of Patmos. I wonder what kinds of thoughts swirled through his mind as the boat returned him to the shores of Asia Minor. I've made this trip by sea, and though it is beautiful, it is not brief. As his thinning gray hair blew across his face, he had time to experience a host of emotions. We have gotten to know him well. What kinds of things do you imagine he thought and felt on the ride back to Ephesus?

John lived to be a very old man. We have no idea how many years he lived beyond his exile. The earliest historians indicate, however, that the vitality of his spirit far exceeded the strength of his frame. His passionate heart continued to beat wildly for the Savior he loved so long. John took personally the words God poured through him. They did not simply run through the human quill and spill on the page. John's entire inner man was indelibly stained by *rhema* ink. In closing, read some of the words obviously inscribed on his heart from that last earthly night with Jesus:

This is My command: love one another as I have loved you. No one has greater love than this, that someone would lay down his life for his friends. You are My friends if you do what I command you. I do not call you slaves anymore, because a slave doesn't know what his master is doing. I have called you friends, because I have made known to you everything I have heard from My Father. You did not choose Me, but I chose you. I appointed you that you should go out and produce fruit and that your fruit should remain, so that whatever you ask the Father in My name, He will give you. This is what I command you: love one another. (John 15:12–17)

> Only disciples who are convinced they are beloved will in turn love beyond themselves. We cannot give what we do not have.

John lived the essence of these verses. He ended his life a true "friend" of Christ, for he took on God's interests as surely as Elisha took on the cloak of Elijah. Early church fathers reported that long after John lacked the strength to walk, younger believers carried the beloved disciple in a chair through crowds gathered for worship. His final sermons were short and sweet: "My little children, love one another!" He poured his life into love. Christ's love. The focus of his final days captures the two concepts I've learned above all others in this journey:

• Christ calls His beloved disciples to forsake ambition for affection. John moved from his "pillar" position in the Jerusalem church to relative obscurity. Better to pour out our lives in places unknown than to become dry bones in the places we've always been.

• Only disciples who are convinced they are beloved will in turn love beyond themselves. Actively embracing the lavish love of God is our only means of extending divine love to injured hearts. We simply cannot give what we do not have.

Don't think for a moment the Savior wasn't nearby when the sounds of an old Son of Thunder grew faint and then silent. After all, John was the solitary remaining apostle who could make the claims of his own pen: "That which was from the beginning, which we have heard, which we have seen with our eyes, which we have looked at and our hands have touched—this we proclaim concerning the Word of life" (1 John 1:1 NIV). "We" had turned to "I," and soon "I" would turn to "they."

Somehow I picture him in his death much like he had been in his life. To me, the scene that captures the beloved disciple most is recorded in John 13:23. The event occurred at a certain table decades earlier. The Amplified Bible says it best. "One of His disciples, whom Jesus loved [whom He esteemed and delighted in] was reclining [next to Him] on Jesus' bosom" (John 13:23). Yes, I like to think that John died just as he lived. Nestled close. Reclining on the breast of an unseen but very present Savior, John's weary head in His tender arms. The Spirit and the bride said, "Come!" And in the distance could be heard a gentle thunder.

Here at the end of our time together, search back through your various journal spaces, and see what God has raised to the top in your mind. What stands out in what He has been saying to you through your experience with Him and with John the beloved? _____

_____

_____

_____

_____

PRAYING GOD'S WORD TODAY

I come at Your invitation, Lord, because I am thirsty for more of You. I desire to take Your living water as a gift into my needy soul. When You testify about all these things, saying, "Yes, I am coming quickly" (Rev. 22:17, 20), my heart has but one thing to answer in response: "Come, Lord Jesus . . ." _____

_____

_____

_____

_____

_____

_____

_____

_____

_____

_____

ENDNOTES

1 R. Alan Culpepper, *John, Son of Zebedee* (Minneapolis: First Fortress Press, 2000), 7.

2 Ronald F. Youngblood and F. F. Bruce, eds. *Nelson's New Illustrated Bible Dictionary* (Nashville: Thomas Nelson, 1999), 473.

3 Matthew Henry, *Matthew to John: Matthew Henry's Commentary on the Whole Bible*, vol. 5 (Grand Rapids: Fleming H. Revell Company, 1985), 456.

4 Frank Gaebelein and J. D. Douglas, *The Expositor's Bible Commentary*, vol. 8 (Grand Rapids: Zondervan Publishing, 1984), 629.

5 Spiros Zodhiates, "Lexical Aids to the Old Testament," #344 in Spiros Zodhiates, Warren Baker, and David Kemp, *Hebrew-Greek Key Study Bible* (Chattanooga, TN: AMG Publishers, 1996), 1503.

6 James Stalker, *The Two St. Johns of the New Testament* (New York: American Tract Society, 1895), 148.

7 Lynn M. Poland, "The New Criticism, Neoorthodoxy, and the New Testament," quoted in Culpepper, *John, Son of Zebedee*, 139.

8 Spiros Zodhiates, *The Complete Word Study Dictionary; New Testament* (Chattanooga, TN: AMG Publishers, 1994), #5485, 1469.

9 Augustine, *Confessions*, trans. R. S. Pine-Coffin (New York: Penguin Books, 1961).

10 Jonathan Edwards, "The End for Which God Created the World," *The Works of Jonathan Edwards* (New York: Yale University Press), 495.

11 C. S. Lewis, *The Weight of His Glory and Other Addresses* (Grand Rapids: Eerdmans, 1965).

12 John Piper, *The Dangerous Duty of Delight* (Sisters, OR: Multnomah Publishers, 2001), 21.

13 Eusebius, quoted in Andreas J. Kostenberger, *Encountering John* (Grand Rapids: Baker Books, 1999), 35.

14 Augustine, quoted in Kostenberger, *Encountering John*, 19.

15 Kostenberger, *Encountering John*, 56.

16 *The Worldbook Encyclopedia 2001*, vol. 8 (Chicago: World Book Inc., 2001), 8–8a.

17 Zodhiates, "Lexical Aids to the Old Testament," #344 in Zodhiates, Baker, and Kemp, *Hebrew-Greek Key Study Bible*, 1437.

18 Zodhiates, *The Complete Word Study Dictionary; New Testament*, #3674, 1046.

19 Ibid., #3670, 1045.

20 "John, A Last Word on Love" *Biblical Illustrator*, Summer 1976, 26.

21 Tertullian, *On Prescription Against Heretics*, as quoted in Culpepper, *John, Son of Zebedee*, 140.

22 Oswald Chambers, *My Utmost for His Highest* (New York: Dodd Mead & Company, 1963), 211.

23 Zodhiates, "Lexical Aids to the New Testament" #918 in Zodhiates, Baker, and Kemp, *Hebrew-Greek Key Study Bible*, 1596.

24 E. Glen Hinson, "Smyrna," *Biblical Illustrator*, Winter 1980, 72, 86.

25 Youngblood and Bruce, *Nelson's New Illustrated Bible Dictionary*, 1187.

26 Taken from *Foxe's Book of Martyrs* by John Foxe, chapter 2, www.biblenet.net/library/foxesMartyrs.

27 A. T. Robertson, *Word Pictures in the New Testament*, vol. 5 (Nashville: Broadman Press, 1960), 307.

28 William Barclay, *Letters to the Seven Churches* (New York: Abingdon, 1957), quoted in *Expositor's*

29 Henry L. Peterson, "The Church at Laodicea," *Biblical Illustrator*, Spring 1982, 74–75.

NOTES

NOTES